Simple Seasons

Simple Seasons

Little Lessons for Large Living

Judi Braddy

© 2006 by Judi Braddy. All rights reserved.
2nd Printing 2014

Trusted Books is an imprint of Deep River Books. The views expressed or implied in this work are those of the author. To learn more about Deep River Books, go online to www.DeepRiverBooks.com.

No part of this publication may be reproduced, stored in a retrieval system or transmitted in any way by any means—electronic, mechanical, photocopy, recording or otherwise—without the prior permission of the copyright holder, except as provided by USA copyright law.

Unless otherwise noted, all Scriptures are taken from the Holy Bible, New International Version, Copyright © 1973, 1978, 1984 by the International Bible Society. Used by permission of Zondervan Publishing House. The "NIV" and "New International Version" trademarks are registered in the United States Patent and Trademark Office by International Bible Society.

Scripture references marked KJV are taken from the King James Version of the Bible.

Scripture references marked NASB are taken from the New American Standard Bible, © 1960, 1963, 1968, 1971, 1972, 1973, 1975, 1977 by The Lockman Foundation. Used by permission.

ISBN: 978-1-63269-123-1
Library of Congress Catalog Card Number: 2006901343

Dedication

Heartfelt thanks to Arlene Allen, Darla Knoth and Peggy Musgrove for providing the original opportunity and encouragement to bring these simple stories to the published page. Great writers in your own right, you are also great friends.

Thanks also to good buddies Jan Coleman and Laura Jensen Walker who have encouraged and edited all along the way, even staying "on call" in spite of personal looming deadlines.

And to my hubby, Jim, who let me off the hook to stay home and write more times than I deserved. Through all life's seasons, I love you.

Table of Contents

From the Author…
   A Few Lightly Seasoned Sentences   ix

SUMMER   15
1. Morning Glories   17
2. Vacation Speculation   20
3. The Pot Thickens   23
4. You're Not From Here, Are You?   26
5. Bats 'R Up!   29
6. A Royal Reunion   32
7. Camp Gramma   35
8. A Stall in the Conversation   38
9. The Convertible   41

AUTUMN   47
1. From Kindergarten to Convertibles   49
2. A Cup of Grace   52

3. Nuts Are People, Too!	55
4. Turkey Time	58
5. Tank 'Ew Much!	61
6. Cross Stitch	64
7. The Purpose Driven Quilt	68
8. Fringe Benefits	71
9. As Time Goes By	74
WINTER	**81**
1. Head Start on the Holidays	84
2. Being Truly Gifted	88
3. The Best Laid Plans	91
4. Why Am I Doing This?	94
5. After the Holidays, the Rest Is Gravy	97
6. Losers, Take Heart	100
7. Photo Opportunity	104
8. A Pearl of Wisdom	108
9. Bah, Flu Bug!	111
SPRING	**117**
1. Growing By Leaps and Bounds	120
2. Spring Cleaning	124
3. Time Change Challenge	127
4. May Mischief	130
5. Happy Mother's Day	133
6. New Lease on Life	137
7. Divine Design	140
8. Squeaky Clean	144
9. The Vernal Pool	147

From the Author… A Few Lightly Seasoned Sentences

King Solomon and I, with only a few centuries in between, have come to the same conclusion. Life is an inevitable cycle full of beginnings and endings. The problem is that sometimes it feels more like we're going in circles than cycles. What, he asks in Ecclesiastes, is the point? Don't we all wonder at times? Here's what *we* decided. God has a season and time for every purpose. Our best hope is to trust His timing, meanwhile living every day to its fullest.

While I don't pretend to possess Solomon's wisdom, I have lived through scads of seasons and turned over a number of new leaves. Here's what I've observed. We often get so busy *living* life that we forget to *look* at life. Yet it's amazing what joy and fulfillment we can find in simple, everyday things—not to mention the important lessons we can learn from them. How? By taking time to notice the hope and humor in nature, human and otherwise, until we inevitably uncover the wisdom rooted in its rhythmic and unfailing cycle of seasons.

Solomon wrote a book about that, too. What a coincidence.

The book you are about to savor, *Simple Seasons: Lighthearted Lessons For Large Living*, is a devotional divided into four seasons containing inspirational stories about everyday things, each with a simple message to stimulate thought. The majority of these stories were previously published in the hope and humor column which I have written for *Woman's Touch Magazine* over the last several seasons. Thus the title. The short commentary and prayer added at the end of each story serves to highlight the most important points, providing a more personal application. Each section concludes with an essay capturing the ambience of that particular season.

Hopefully these insights will tug at the memories, hearts, and souls of those in all seasons of life's journey. The stories are simple, but even Solomon's wisdom was illustrated as often by ants and plants as by people and palaces. If they can remind us that nothing is an accident with God, but part of the plan He long ago set in motion; that each season prepares us for the next as we are strengthened by its lessons; and that through every season God is faithful, this book will have found its own season and purpose.

From the Author...
A Few Lightly Seasoned Sentences

Perhaps nothing sums it up as well as the following verse and chorus from a favorite hymn:[1]

"Summer and winter and springtime and harvest,
Sun, moon and stars in their courses above.
Join with all nature in manifold witness
To Thy great faithfulness, mercy and love.
Great is Thy faithfulness, great is Thy faithfulness
Morning by morning new mercies I see.
All I have needed Thy hand hath provided
Great is Thy faithfulness, Lord unto me.

---

[1] Thomas O. Chisholm, *Great Is Thy Faithfulness*, (Singspiration, Inc. 1974) 40.

*Summer afternoon—summer afternoon;
to me those have always been the most beautiful words
in the English language.*
—Henry James

SUMMER

Who doesn't love summer? It's the time of vacations, lemonade stands and finding cool ways to beat the heat. It's also the season during which conditions are just right and growth takes place rapidly. How natural it seems to simply take it easy and enjoy. My advice? Don't feel about guilty laying down a responsibility or two for a lazy lounge in the hammock or a picnic in the park. Kick back, enjoy and make the most of those long, languid days. We all know they don't last forever.

There are summers in our spiritual life, as well, when in the most easy and natural way God seems to be growing us by leaps and bounds. He brings friends and fellowship to encourage us, provides lessons laced with love and laughter, allows us to simply sit back and enjoy the journey. Seems we have only to bask in the warmth. *If this is what liv-*

ing the Christian life is all about, we think, *keep it comin', Lord.*

Only one problem. These seasons can't last forever, either. When growth takes place too easily and rapidly, we tend to take too much for granted. Like a verdant vine, things can quickly cultivate out of control.

We all know it's not uncommon during this sizzling season to experience the occasional heat wave. As the thermometer climbs, the climate can get quite uncomfortable. Then it takes special care along with a little extra irrigation if things are to continue to grow. When things get really hot, experts tell us the best way to avoid heat stroke is to use caution and common sense.

Likewise in our Christian lives, there are times when God may choose to turn up the heat a bit. Then, wan and wilting, we have but one wise choice: seek out the cool pastures of prayer and the still water of his word. Just a quick dip and we'll soon find ourselves refreshed and restored.

So, whether you are basking or baking, here to help are a few stories illustrating Christian growth in a summer setting.

CHAPTER ONE

Morning Glories

...for his compassions never fail. They are new every morning. Great is your faithfulness.
—Lamentations 3:22-23

Summer's in full swing, which means long before I open my eyes each morning the sun is up. So, invariably, is my husband. As long as I've known him, he has always been a morning person. To tell the truth, I'm never sure which of the two gets up first. Why? I am NOT a morning person.

As such, I'll never understand how people can spring out of bed, not just wide awake but with enthusiasm akin to water at a full boil. Maybe that's why their first task is to turn on the shower, producing the sound and steam of a jungle rainforest. Somehow it also induces singing. Or humming. Or a combination of the two. *Great is Thy faithfulness, hum…hum…Thy faithfulness. Morning by hum… hum…* You get the idea.

Inevitably at some point they will also turn on an overhead light.

In this super-imposed state of early bird euphoria they simply don't seem aware of any reason the rest of us might not share their enthusiasm. Contrary to unflattering commentary and cartoon caricatures, we are not grumpy or ungrateful people. We start the day the same way they do—just later and slower.

One more thing. If you live with a reticent riser, it may pay to remember that on the occasions when we must get up early, the fact that we are walking and talking does not mean we are awake or ready to function.

Here's the good news. Early or otherwise, Lamentations 3:22-23 tells us that God's compassions never fail. They are new every morning. Now if you exuberant early birds could just show a little of the same.

Be bright. Show your enthusiasm for each new day. But for the rest of our sakes take a lesson from morning glories. They are bright, too, yet no one knows exactly what time their vibrant trumpets open to catch the early dew. Why?

They do it quietly.

We are grateful, Lord, for your new mercies each morning. Quiet mercies.

Turning Over A New Leaf

Even for those of us who are less enthusiastic about getting up early, I have to admit that there's something about a summer morning that makes it somewhat easier. Perhaps it's the sunlight streaming through the window, the beauty of everything in full bloom, or the fact that the birds and bees are already up and busily buzzing about. No matter how long (or short) the night, things look completely different in the light of a fresh, new day.

Then there's the appeal of enjoying those few early hours before the heat hits full strength. Whatever it takes to get us up and going, it's a great time to develop the habit of having a quiet time with the Lord. Sitting under the gazebo with an open Bible and a fresh cup of coffee—now there's something worth waking up for.

Thank you, Lord, for the gift of each new morning. Your grace and mercy are written all over it. Pull us fully awake so that we can say with the Psalmist, "In the morning, O Lord, you hear my voice; in the morning I lay my requests before you and wait in expectation." Amen.

CHAPTER TWO

Vacation Speculation

> In all your ways acknowledge him, and he will make your paths straight.
> —Proverbs 3:6

The weather is warm, the kids are out of school—it's time for that most enjoyable, much anticipated, but highly overrated activity: The Summer Vacation.

Ever wonder who started this grand tradition? Well, Scripture is a little sketchy, but a number of clues point to Moses. Consider some suspicious similarities.

For months God and Moses had been going over the plans for the Israelites' little excursion into the wilderness. Speculation has it this may well have included a map because, to this very day, there's hardly a man alive without a library of 'em. Just mention a trip and out they come! Oh, the measuring and muttering—just to find the longest route with the fewest rest stops. Hmmm. Makes you wonder about that Red Sea incident, doesn't it? Is it possible that even God might resort to the miraculous just to avoid unnecessary detours?

Then there was Pharaoh's early morning wake-up call to Moses. This surely explains why certain folks still think it's imperative to be packed and on the road before the crack of dawn. And speaking of packing...if the Israelites hadn't been in such an all-fired hurry, we might not be rushing to the airport now with only two bags and a carry-on. Think about it.

This Biblical account certainly confirms one well-known fact. No one leaves on vacation without forgetting something. Why else would the Israelites have asked the Egyptians for clothes and accessories on their way out of town? Two miles down the road someone was undoubtedly heard to say "I wonder if I left the oil lamp burning..."

So much for silly speculation. Still it's a comfort to know that no matter where your journey takes you, God goes before you. The one lesson that leaves little latitude is the importance of staying with his plan in order to avoid unnecessary detours. Moses would tell you. Forty years is a lo-o-ong trip, and it wasn't any vacation.

Turning Over A New Leaf

Anyone who's ever been on an extended family vacation knows. They can be highly overrated.

The more people you have, the more complicated things can become. Haven't we all heard the term "traveling mercies"? No doubt about it. We should always include God in any travel plans we make, asking him for patience and direction. Remember, too, that wherever life's journey takes us, we all have a divine destination. It's the lessons we learn and the memories we make along the way that will help us arrive safely and joyfully. Let's just hope we're faster learners and better remember-ers than the Israelites.

> *Lord, thank you for special times of fun with family, of rest and relaxation. Help us make the most of them. Give us patience in the process, joy in the journey and wisdom all along the way. May we remember to follow your divine direction so that the memories we make will last not only for a lifetime, but for eternity as well. Amen.*

CHAPTER THREE

The Pot Thickens

Two are better than one because they have a good reward for their work.
—Ecclesiastes 4:9

"You've gotta be kidding!" My husband, Jim, glared at the humongous clay flower pot towering in the back of our SUV. It had taken four guys at the outdoor market to load it; frankly, I hadn't thought about how we'd get it out. I was too excited to find the identical pot which sells at a local nursery for twice the price. Decorated with lemons, it was perfect for that empty back yard corner.

"Back yard!! You want us to carry it to the back yard?!" Why does this man invariably put a damper on my enthusiasm? His frown told me I'd better devise a plan quickly. My solution: enlist our son and next door neighbor, Bob.

This, of course, meant the first plan of action would be the prerequisite male strategy discussion. Then, as I hovered anxiously, the three guys wrestled Mt. Terra Cotta into my dad's old wheelbarrow. Red-faced, my husband pushed as the other two balanced. Finally...progress.

Three steps later the wheel collapsed.

Any momentary bubble of sentiment I had for the wheelbarrow burst with Jim's next words. "Well, for Pete's sake, we can't just leave it here." Thank goodness for Pete, whoever he is.

Finally they tipped the wheelbarrow low enough to roll the clay boulder out. Roll? "It rolls!" Bob yelled. "Let's roll it the rest of the way." Great idea. I watched the 3-D lemons being flattened by the concrete. Not such a great idea.

Bob's remedy then was to slide it on a rug, one whose rubber backing was less than conducive. Next, a large piece of cardboard placed underneath showed promise. Except it kept slipping. So for the last few feet my husband and son pulled while Bob ran in circles repositioning the rug. At the appointed destination, it took all three guys to heave the pot onto its final resting place.

Still, scratches and all, the pot looks great. Though yesterday I noticed it's crowding two bay trees. I wonder how long I should wait before suggesting to my husband the tree relocation project.

Turning Over A New Leaf

How could such a simple garden project end up involving and exhausting so many people? Even with the best intentions life has a way of becoming unexpectedly complicated—admittedly, sometimes due to poor planning. How blessed we are to have family and friends who aide and abet us through these experiences, even when it's a pain in the flower pot. *Real friendship*, states Abraham Kuyper, *is shown in time of trouble; prosperity is full of friends.* So true.

A small tree now lives in that large pot. I never look at it without a contemplative chuckle and a grateful heart for the people who made it possible, even managing to share some reflective laughs later over a glass of cold lemonade.

Lord, thank you for flower pots, family and friends. You use so many things in our lives to teach, touch and bless us. We're grateful. Grant us all an extra portion of patience the next time someone needs our help. It might help, too, if you'd provide us impetuous souls with a smidge more foresight. Amen

CHAPTER FOUR

You're Not From Here, Are You?

Stop judging by mere appearance, and make a right judgment.
—John 7:24

The name of the resort, Journey's End, about summed it up.

We'd snaked forty miles off the interstate through tall pines and mountain passes to reach the remote church where my husband, Jim, would be speaking the next morning. *Thank goodness we've made hotel reservations,* I thought. Finally we spied the faded sign and swerved in, dust and gravel flying.

This was it?

The 'resort' consisted of a rustic bait shop, restaurant/saloon and grocery, whose checkout counter doubled as the hotel check-in. Our concierge, uniformed in a 1998 Bass Derby t-shirt, thumbed through a dog-eared calendar, and then grabbed a walkie-talkie. Jim and I exchanged nervous glances. A few spits and crackles later he handed us a key marked #4.

"Rooms are up the hill. Store's open 'til nine. Have a nice stay."

Okey-dokey then.

With only four rooms, #4 was pretty easy to find—even without the door distinguished by peeling paint. Despite the rough exterior, though, everything was clean, much to my relief. One thing was for sure. The quiet isolation—i.e. no phone or TV—promised a restful night's sleep.

"Well," Jim said after we'd settled, "where would you like to dine?" We dissolved into giggles.

Next morning a pleasant waitress filled our coffee mugs, then, eyeing our Sunday attire, spoke the obvious.

"You're not from here, are you?"

A family of boaters and two guys in hunters' camouflage, turned to listen. Seems conversation in that neck-o'-the-woods was like deer season. Open game. Soon we'd been updated on weather, wildlife, and other woodsy wonders. It wasn't until one of the camouflage guys came around with coffee that I realized we were actually enjoying the colorful company.

Later, halfway to church, the waitress's words echoed back. "You're not from here, are you?" That's when the truth hit me. None of us are. We're just passing through. And if we're not careful, we could miss some interesting and amazing people, places and experiences because we don't take time to look past a few rough exteriors.

Not a bad thought to ponder this side of Journey's End.

Turning Over A New Leaf

How many times have we found ourselves put off by someone's appearance or repulsed by a less-than-desirable set of circumstances? Our only thought at that moment might be to retrace our tracks and climb back into our own cushy little comfort zone. Yet if we're willing to linger a little longer and dig a little deeper, we might find a treasure chest full of new experiences and interesting eccentricities. So next time you're tempted to make a snap judgment, take a moment to reconsider. Could be God has caused you to veer off the well-worn path for a heavenly purpose.

Lord, deliver us from snap judgments. There are people and places out there just waiting to be discovered—people you love in places you created despite the outward appearance of either. Give us eyes to look beyond the rough exterior so that we can see both the internal and eternal treasure. Amen.

CHAPTER FIVE

Bats 'R Up!

To all perfection I see a limit, but your commands are boundless.
—Psalm 119:96

Vacation in paradise... The travel brochure had done its seductive duty. Now my husband, Jim, and I sat sipping fresh fruit punch from tall, frosty glasses at the Fijian island resort. A long way to travel? Yes, but worth it to be alone on our own tropical island. Never mind those fifty other guests. A few feet away gentle waves nibbled the toes of a white sand beach. Palm fronds rustled in the balmy breeze. Island birds flitted from tree to tree. Ahhh... the sounds of paradise.

Just then something resembling a stealth bomber flapped across the sky, glided over the pool area, and disappeared.

"Did you see the size of that bird?" I said.

Jim squinted to see where it had landed. "Yeah, only it wasn't a bird."

"It was flying, what else could it be?"

"It was a bat."

No doubt my eyes resembled the pineapple ring garnishing my glass. "Bat? The vacation brochure never mentioned bats!"

"Maybe you missed that page." Was he smirking? "Bats are natural inhabitants of these islands. Evening is their feeding time." He *was* smirking. One paltry pamphlet and the man's convinced he's a winged-mammal master.

But he was right. By the time the sun plunged fluorescent into the sea, we'd sighted several. And heard more. Seems the brochure had also failed to describe the noise bats make in a feeding frenzy—something reminiscent of cats with their tails tied together, flung across a clothes line.

So much for the sounds of paradise.

Bats notwithstanding, we finished our vacation and had a wonderful time. Still, the creepy creatures served to remind us that no paradise this side of heaven is perfect. Nor is the grass necessarily greener on the other side of the island. Consequently, by week's end we were both ready to come home and scout out a few local bats before summer's end. The kind viewed over a hot dog at the local baseball stadium.

Turning Over A New Leaf

At least once a year, most of us get stressed with our own surroundings and start searching for the perfect place to get away from it all. That's what vacations are all about. Thankfully, God has created some incredible places here on earth to choose from. Still, no matter how wonderful the change of scenery, no place is perfect. Usually by the end we're more than ready to go home.

The same will be true some day of our time on earth. Here's the good news. Jesus is already preparing a perfect place for us, which he describes in John 14, a heavenly house with many rooms. And according to the "travel brochure", not only will he leave the light on for us, but airfare is included.

Lord, thank you for the many amazing places you've created on earth for our enjoyment. We are truly blessed by the opportunities you provide for travel and times of relaxation with family and friends. As wonderful as these times are, we can only try to imagine what heaven will be like. All we can say is "Wish you were here—see you soon." Amen.

CHAPTER SIX

A Royal Reunion

Now I know in part, then I shall know fully, even as I am fully known.
—I Corinthians 13:12

Wondering what happened to all your old friends? A summer reunion is being planned...

The words played across the invitation like a nostalgic tune on the oldies station. These were Christian comrades from my high school youth choir.

"I can hardly wait!" I chirped to my husband.

"Think you'll recognize each other?"

"What do you mean? People don't change that much in. . .

Thirty-five years. Yikes.

I dashed to my closet. Surely there was one outfit that made me look younger. And thinner.

A few weeks later I stood nervously outside the designated destination, an aging photo album wedged under one arm. Tucking in my tummy, I opened the door.

Inside milled a mélange of middle-agers. Who were these people? *Oops*, I decided, *wrong room*. Just as I turned to leave, an excited southern accent cut across the room. "Judi, is that y'all?"

Sans my age-revealing spectacles, I squinted in the direction of the drawl. "Sally? Sally Spencer?!" Under a fancy new frost job a familiar face bobbed toward me. Thus began a joyous rush of repeated recognition.

Much food and fraternizing later, the whole gregarious group circled to reminisce. Seems from our blended beginnings life had scattered us across some interesting, uncharted territory. The accounts ranged from hopeful to heartbreaking to flat-out hilarious. Sally, for instance, had married and moved to Mississippi to help run the family farm. When her husband died unexpectedly, all she'd inherited was a southern drawl. But with the help of friends, she started a small baking business—one that now ships worldwide.

Story after story, two themes prevailed: God's faithfulness and the blessing of friendships. Basking in the glow of reclaimed relationships, it struck me. This is only a sampling of the stories we'll share in heaven. Suddenly the words from the invitation marched back with new meaning. *Wondering what happened to all your old friends? A reunion is being planned...*

A royal reunion! With no worries about what to wear.

Turning Over A New Leaf

Reunions can be both fun and fretful as we contemplate who might be there and what changes time may have brought. The delightful discovery is that, as part of God's family, no matter how long it's been, we can just take up where we left off. Seems with God, we always have something in common. The really neat thing is that though he takes us in many diverse directions, they'll all eventually lead us home to Heaven. What a royal reunion that will be.

> *Lord, thank you for the friends you have woven into our lives over the years. Though some are only for a season, in your pattern, all are for a reason. What a serendipitous surprise when you allow our paths to unexpectedly cross this side of heaven. Yet what a greater and more glorious joy it will be when we are reunited forever in heaven. Consider this my RSVP. Amen.*

CHAPTER SEVEN

Camp Gramma

He who fears the Lord has a secure fortress and for his children it will be a refuge.
—Proverbs 14:26

When first learning that we were going to be grandparents, I had four words to say: "Let the games begin!"

I love being a (very young) gramma. To my way of thinking, it's maximum fun with minimum responsibility. Yessiree. Gramma's my name...spoiling is my game.

That's why, anticipating a week's vacation with all four grands, I spent days transforming our backyard into a summer camp complete with tent, cots and sleeping bags. The barbeque became a campfire for cooking burgers, dogs and s'mores. From build-a-bear to bowling, daily activities were painstakingly planned. The hand-painted sign tacked on the gazebo said it all:

CAMP GRAMMA.

So imagine my surprise that first evening to find them all camped out in front of the TV, four pairs of grizzly bear slippers protruding at odd angles from wall-to-wall sleeping bags.

"How come you guys aren't out in the tent?"

"We like it in here," chirped the oldest.

"It-th dark and th-cary out there," lisped the youngest.

"Nonsense. Grampa promised he'd ...say, where is Grampa?"

As if on cue, a loud snore erupted from a large, blanketed lump near-by.

Deserter.

"Okay," I conceded. "Now let's hit the hay. Tomorrow's gonna be busy."

"Gramma," a sleepy voice drifted from the bunched-up bedding, "will you tell us a Bible story?"

"And don't forget to remember our prayers," called another contented camper.

It had been our bedtime routine for every visit. How could I "forget to remember?"

Later, watching them sleep, a warm truth snuggled its way in. Being a Christian grandparent is much more than fun and games. It includes planting spiritual seeds, instilling self-confidence and providing a safe place when the world gets dark and "th-cary".

Proverbs 14:26 promises, "He who fears the Lord has a secure fortress and for his children (and their children) it will be a refuge."

A fortress and refuge—that's Camp Gramma. Where memories are made not only for a lifetime, but eternity.

Let the games begin.

Turning Over A New Leaf

Being a Christian grandparent is more than just fun and wonderful. It involves playing an important spiritual role as well. For our children and grandchildren we provide a link to the past, an anchor in the present, and a lifeline to the future. We have learned from our own parenting mistakes and, as a result, have the experience that gives us both patience and perspective. Because we don't have to be the disciplinarians, we can offer something that parents often cannot: objectivity. In Deuteronomy 4:9, God, speaking of what the Israelites have seen, instructs: "Teach them to your children and to their children after them." Now I ask you. How many times in life do we get a second chance to do it right?

> *Lord, thank you for our grandchildren, for the joy and assurance they bring that, regardless of our success or failure, something of us will live on. Help us to be wise and loving in our delicate dealings with them that we might leave a lasting godly legacy. While we live, may we provide a refuge of safety in an uncertain world. Amen.*

CHAPTER EIGHT

A Stall in the Conversation

...and his sheep follow him because they know his voice.

—John 10:4

Is it just me, or have you also noticed? The more advanced our tools of communication become, the more common courtesy seems to be going...excusé moi ...right down the toilette.

A story from my friend Dar Rossi is a perfect case in point.

Every woman knows that one of the best escapes from the summer heat is a trip to an air-conditioned mall. During such an extended shopping spree, Dar found herself in urgent need of the ladies room. No sooner had she settled in a stall when she was startled by a vivacious voice coming from next door.

"Hi, there!"

Composing herself, Dar managed a weak "hello."

"How ya doin'?" the voice chirped.

"Ff-fine."

"How's the family?"

"Uh, doing quite well, thanks," ventured Dar, still a bit suspicious of this sociable stranger.

"Well, I tell ya...it's been quite a week at our house..." and for nearly a minute the anonymous annotator elaborated as Dar, in her less-than-commodious confines, offered polite interjections. Then the conversation took a confounding curve.

"Can you hang on just a minute, Mildred?" continued the covert conversationalist.

Mildred. Who's Mildred?

"Someone in the next stall keeps talking and I can't hear a word you're saying."

Reality registered in a flush...er, flash. Seems the bathroom blabber had been on her cell phone the entire time.

While Dar's embarrassing encounter makes for a side-splitting story, it also contains a resonating ring for us all. Seems we can't go anywhere nowadays without falling victim to a vast variety of voices vying for our time and attention. How can we possibly sort them all out?

A passage in John 10 comes to mind, warning of those who come in the back door of the sheepfold to confuse and divide. Thankfully, the faithful Shepherd is there keeping watch. "And his sheep follow him," it concludes, "because they know his voice."

Don't want to be confused by a stranger in the next stall? Take a daily detour during this sizzling season to the cool pastures and still waters. It's only there that we become unflinchingly familiar with the Shepherd's voice.

And here's some additional advice from Dar. Next time you hear nature calling, think twice before answering.

Turning Over A New Leaf

From TV to telephone to Internet, never have there been so many venues for information and conversation. We simply must weigh the words we hear carefully. Even then, it's easy to be confused and bemused. No wonder it's so important that we get in the habit of taking time early each day to tune our ears and hearts to the right frequency. Then, before we respond to, or worse, repeat something we've heard, ask the Lord to give us wisdom.

Lord, sometimes it seems that all we can hear are the voices around us. Too often, yours is the hardest for us to hear. Perhaps you are quiet so that we must press in, learning to tune out the voices around us and finding the frequency of your voice alone. Maybe you are not quiet at all; we are just not listening loud enough. Amen.

CHAPTER NINE

The Convertible

...let us throw off everything that hinders and the sin that so easily entangles...and let us run with perseverance the race marked out for us.
—Hebrews 12:1

My husband and I bought a convertible today, a shiny red one with power everything. Granted it is last year's model and served as a rental car for a year, so there are a few scratches—which is why we got an amazing deal and finally bought it.

You see, the idea of having a convertible has mostly been a fantasy of mine over the last few years, even a joke at times between my husband, Jim, and me. Sort of like the Harley he's going to buy someday, a big one we can just jump on and go wherever and whenever we feel the urge. Without room for a lot of baggage, it would be just we two and our toothbrushes.

Yes we've joked about the convertible. Yet more and more lately I found myself looking at every convertible that passed us on the road, always trying to catch a glimpse of the driver. *Do I fit the image?* I wondered. To my amazement, I discovered convertible drivers come in all shapes, sizes and ages, but a lot of them look my age and older.

Maybe that was part of my problem. I guess at my age driving a convertible seemed to me a wee bit too closely connected with a mid-life crisis. And another thing—they're not very practical. What about safety? You roll one of those babies with the top down and it's all over. I have too many responsibilities to take a risk like that.

Responsibilities. Let's face it, no one lives without incurring some excess baggage. Homes with mortgages, credit cards with monthly payments, children with down payments and upkeep, aging parents with failing health—just to mention a few.

Could it be that to some extent the cars we drive represent stages of our lives? Take, for instance, the first car we bought as newlyweds: a 1967 Firebird with four-speed transmission. Teaching me to drive that car was one of the first true tests of our marriage. A few years later we "muscled up" to a GTO which we drove until our first child and a move to Alaska made a Plymouth station wagon a necessity. What a drastic change in life and limo that was. I'm not sure Jim has ever fully recovered from that trade. I know neither of us has fully recovered from that child.

Summer

Over the years followed a succession of family cars and vans that transported a variety of kids, equipment and groceries. Then one by one our three boys began to drive and we had to help them buy cars. Now, finally, we are down to one part-time kid and two fuel-efficient cars consisting of a company vehicle and a small, semi-sporty compact.

Until today, that is.

Just a few hours ago the salesman, still perspiring from the haggle with my husband over the terms of the sale—it's a guy thing—handed me the keys to the convertible. We reviewed all the bells and whistles then, with the top down but windows up, I pulled cautiously out of the car lot and turned the corner. The light turned green. As we picked up a little speed, I decided to throw caution to the wind—literally—and roll down all the windows. Beginning to feel myself relax as the summer breeze gently restyled my hair, I quickly stole a look at the passenger seat. My husband, I discovered, had turned his baseball hat backwards on his head. He glanced over and we smiled at each other with a look reflecting the sudden realization that maybe, just maybe, we had turned more than just an asphalt corner.

We can't give up the company car yet, but it's interesting how we are already looking for places to drive the convertible. Sure, we still have responsibilities, but it's almost as if putting the top down allows any pressing or unreasonable worries to blow away, even if only temporarily.

Oh, and one more thing. While some may fail to appreciate the design of a convertible that necessitates a small trunk, I already see a value in it. After all, it will force us to take along only what is most important. In fact, I suppose the only vehicle with less room for baggage is probably, well, a Harley.

Hmmm?

*The creation of a thousand forests
is in one acorn.*
—Henry James

AUTUMN

Something in the air tells you that change is coming. First, you wake to a noticeable morning chill. Soon the days are getting cooler and crisper and the leaves begin to change color. Walking down the street one day, a sudden brisk breeze causes a kaleidoscopic cascade. The shorter days and longer shadows give rise to reflection—a tool, perhaps, for accepting the unstoppable transition that is taking place. Before you know it, the branches are mostly bare, only a few brave bits holding on for dear life. All that remains of summer is a dust-and-dry-leaf scent.

Like autumn at its peak, life changes can also be exciting and exhilarating, often producing a new brilliance, a clearer and crisper outlook. Sometimes, though, the circumstances around us can swirl too fast, making us dizzy and indecisive. In some cases, everything that we've held dear seems to be stripped away. Is it any wonder that many people don't care much for change, finding it unsettling and disruptive? If you are one of those, here's a thought that may help.

Though we all enjoy the brilliant array of fall colors, few of us understand the process that produces that glorious display. As days grow shorter, trees produce less green chlorophyll causing leaves to reveal their natural, spectacular color. In the same way, change has a way of bringing out our own true colors. It is often the autumns of our lives, when all pretenses are finally stripped away, that our most vivid colors show.

And you thought leaves were supposed to be green.

Embrace it or not, change will come to all of us at one time or another. Or as someone else put it, "The only thing in life that is certain is change." Believe me, after thirty-eight years of marriage and ministry involving twenty-six moves and producing three grown sons and five beautiful grandchildren, I know. The thing that has helped me most in our many shifts and cycles is to focus not on what changes in life, but on what remains constant. James 1:17 is a scripture that has taken me through a lot of transitions: "Every good and perfect gift is from above, coming down from the Father of the heavenly lights, who does not change like shifting shadows."

Now for some stories which, with a wood-smoked tinge of nostalgia, illustrate spiritual growth in life's changing seasons. Hopefully you'll be encouraged to let go of the branch and enjoy the ride.

CHAPTER ONE

From Kindergarten to Convertibles

Train a child in the way he should go, and when he is old he will not turn from it.
—Proverbs 22:6

The square, bent-edged photo captures me in the driveway of our small 1950's frame house in Wichita, Kansas. I am wearing too-short bangs, a too-long dress, white ankle socks and clutching my new school binder. First-day-of-school excitement and apprehension give me a goofy expression—as if the bangs and ankle socks weren't enough. What could my mother have been thinking?

Fast forward. I gaze through the 1970's-style picture window framed by orange drapes, a toddler at my side and baby on my hip. My oldest, balancing a backpack three-fourths his size, marches bravely toward the big yellow bus. He's eager for kindergarten. I'm not. As the bus pulls away, his face presses against the window, bearing that reminiscent goofy look. I should have kept him back a year. What could I have been thinking?

Life, it seems, is a continuous cycle of learning. From the "book learnin'", as grandma called it, through the plethora of practicalities gleaned from awful but adjustable errors in judgment—like too-short bangs, white socks and orange drapes. Hard lessons come as well, swirling like dry leaves on a September breeze, some tinged with frosty regret. Would another year of maturity have helped my eldest son make better choices later in life?

Some things we'll never know.

It is then we must learn life's most important lesson: to trust the all-knowing One. In God's great textbook Professor Solomon illustrates this lesson: "The fear of the Lord is the beginning of wisdom and knowledge of the Holy One is understanding." (Proverbs 9:10)

So the cycle of learning continues. That baby on my hip in the '70s is now bound for college. As we wave him out of the driveway en route to our Midwestern alma mater, my tears begin to flow. Life and learning seem to have come full-circle.

But that's not why I'm crying.

He is driving my red convertible. Lord, what could I have been thinking?

Turning Over A New Leaf

One of the scriptures most often served to Christian parents on a promise platter is Proverbs 22:6.

Some see it as a guarantee. IF we train our children, THEN they won't turn away. Certainly seems like a foolproof formula, doesn't it? The part that's a bit hard to digest is that little phrase "when he is old", indicating that in some cases we might have to wait awhile. As Christians we train our children by instilling scriptural values, sharing knowledge and experience, and providing opportunities for Christian education. The rest, very simply, belongs to God.

Are you anxious about your children's well-being and future? Do you have children who have turned from faith? Keep dropping those time capsules of truth into their lives. I can guarantee you this. God will never let them forget.

> *Lord, we thank you for your holy Word which you promise will never return void. Hide it not only in our hearts, but our children's as well. We commit them once again to you by name, asking that you guard and protect them even as you complete your cycle of learning in their lives. Amen.*

CHAPTER TWO

A Cup of Grace

And God is able to make all grace abound to you, so that in all things at all times, having all that you need, you will abound in every good work.
—II Corinthians 9:8

"Poor confused dear" I said to myself. "She's given me a cup with someone else's name on it." I raised the rustic pottery mug, complete with cider mix, from its spice-scented gift bag. Cream colored with rich brown accents, embossed with autumn leaves, it had one word painted on it: *Grace*. Silly me, it was meant to be inspirational. Then I knew my friend was confused. I have some good qualities, but graceful? I don't think so.

Still, it's interesting how someone else's expectations raise your own. Drinking out of that mug, I felt truly special. More graceful and...slim. How is it that those two things always seem related?

Two months later I kicked it out of the car and broke it. Way to go, Grace!

It was an accident, of course. I had absentmindedly put the empty cup on the floorboard near my foot, and then opened the door. As if in slow motion it fell and someone—could it be me?—squeaked "oh, no". A half-second later, Grace became a two-syllable word.

I felt terrible. I had started to believe that hopeful, redeeming message described me. Unfortunately I forgot to inform my foot. Ah, such irony. How would I tell my friend I had destroyed her beautiful mug? Now she would know I in no way matched its thoughtful inscription. Just when I needed grace the most, it was broken.

Broken grace? Thank goodness there is a difference between being graceful and full of grace. One is related to walking naturally, the other spiritually. Gracefulness is learned, but God's grace is a gift we can never break. He loves us despite mistakes, forgives shortcomings before we admit them, and teaches us to do the same for others. We're talking grace for the grace challenged.

Will my friend have that kind of grace? Yes. She will forgive and still love me, klutz that I am. Maybe she will even buy me a new mug. My guess is it will be plastic.

Turning Over A New Leaf

Ever worry that you'll use up your allowance of grace? The above scripture is only one of many references Paul made to grace in his writings. If anyone knew what it was to stand in need of grace, it was the Apostle Paul. In affluence and affliction, he reiterated his reliance on God's grace, encouraging his readers to do the same.

We've all heard the term "grace under fire." Perhaps the most amazing thing about grace is that the more we appropriate it, the more likely it will spill over in the tough times. Not only is God's grace sufficient, it is never in short supply. This means we, too, can be grace-givers. Know someone who needs your gift of grace? It only takes a minute to give, but can make an eternity of difference.

Thank you, Lord, for your unfailing grace and mercy in our lives. How we depend on it; but don't let us be grace guzzlers. Help us to look for ways each day to lavish it on others. Perhaps that one small glimpse of grace will open someone's eyes to your own vast grace and mercy. Amen.

CHAPTER THREE

Nuts Are People, Too!

But each man has his own gift from God, one has this gift, another has that.
—I Corinthians 7:7

Now that we're into our second season, I feel we know each other well enough to risk sharing a deep, dark secret. I am a leaf and nut person.

Before someone draws an unflattering conclusion, let me clarify. Not just every nut attracts my attention, though some of my best friends are...well, never mind. I am particularly drawn to the nut of the oak—acorns, that is. Thus, I have a hard time resisting anything painted, printed, plastered or pressed displaying leaves or acorns.

A few years ago I ordered a custom-built hutch. For uniqueness, I instructed the cabinet maker to cut out oak leaves and acorns on the center panel. What he delivered was something that resembled six-fingered hands extending toward tiny tops. Thankfully, he had simply installed the panel upside down and was able to reverse it. This, however, illustrates a solitary but significant truth: it's extremely important that nuts be pointed in the right direction.

Autumn is the season which makes many of us go completely—pardon the pun—nuts. Understandably so. Spring has its burgeoning buds, summer its shimmering shade, but autumn has the last brilliant "yippee!" Leaves crunch, rustle and swish. A brisk breeze produces a kaleidoscopic cacophony of color. (Try saying that three times real fast!) Frosty mornings generate a nostalgic waft of wood-smoked memories, often resulting in an undignified romp through someone's leaf pile. Of course, those who develop a cacophony of fall allergies are understandably less enthusiastic. Not to mention the irate leaf-rakers.

Sadly, some see autumn's brilliance as only the transient precursor to a season of bleakness. But pause to reflect more closely and you'll observe its tapestry of latent promise. Pick up a leaf. Examine the intricacy of the edges, veins and stems. God made each one unique and special. Under each tiny, scalloped acorn turret lays the potential for another mighty oak.

Yup. It's quite possible there's more to us leaf and nut people than one might imagine.

Turning Over A New Leaf

As the old saying goes: "Different strokes for different folks". Still, sometimes we have a hard time understanding why people have certain tastes, ideas and interests—especially if they are very different than our own. Quite simply, what appeals to one does not always appeal to another. Personally I find this refreshing. After all, wouldn't it be boring if we all looked and thought alike?

Certainly there were no more diverse personalities and interests than those of the twelve disciples, a group comprised of fishermen, tax collectors, zealots, even a traitor—or two, if you count Peter's moment of weakness. Yet Jesus chose them on purpose, knowing it would be this rough rabble, this vast variety who could build his church. I don't know about you, but that gives me hope that he sees something of value in me as well. Now if we could only learn to lay aside our preconceived ideas and prejudices long enough to accept, even come to appreciate the diversity in each other. Perhaps it will help to remember that different though we may be we are all precious to God.

> *Lord, help us. We are like the blind man in the Bible who, when first touched, saw men only "as trees walking." We need a second touch to see "all things as Jesus saw them." Give us not just sight, but insight to love and accept others the way you love and accept them. Let that be the real difference others see in us. Amen.*

CHAPTER FOUR

Turkey Time

No discipline seems pleasant at the time, but painful. Later on, however, it produces a harvest of righteousness and peace...
—Hebrews 12:11

Let's talk turkey. Did you ever wonder how it became the official holiday bird? After all, Benjamin Franklin once nominated the turkey as our national emblem instead of the eagle. I suspect he lost because someone observed that even a large eagle would never feed twenty people, then provide three months of soup, sandwiches and casseroles. And can you imagine a turkey atop the flag pole?

Consequently, ninety-five percent of the nation participates in the annual turkey trot, intently circling a frozen meat case containing what resembles beige boulders with handlebars. The turkey veterans are easily identified by gloved hands, while novices blow on bare, frost bitten fingers. If you are the latter, here's some advice. When you spot the perfect bird, never make eye contact lest someone jump your claim. Then, once staked, have the butcher maneuver it into your shopping cart. This requires a small crane and you don't want to drop one of those gobblers on your foot. Trust me, I know.

At home you'll need manpower or a good wheelbarrow in transferring from car to kitchen. Only then will you discover that no way is Tom Troublemaker going to fit into your freezer. You might consider leaving him on the counter, except the directions warn that thawing must take place in the refrigerator. In which case, plan on turkey for Easter.

Face it. Turkeys are a pain in the gizzard. Yet, finally thawed, I always experience a moment of pre-stuffing reverence viewing that naked, goosebumply bird. Soon he'll emerge from the oven transformed—the crispy, bronze focal point of another wonderful family celebration, all prior preparation shadowed in the glow of those loving faces.

Hebrews 12:11 indicates that every discipline of life seems, in the preparation stages, more painful than pleasant (my paraphrase). But in the end it produces an amazing "harvest of righteousness and peace."

Whether it's the holidays, or some random Tuesday, that's something it might pay to remember the next time you wrestle a turkey.

Turning Over A New Leaf

I can still remember the first turkey I ever cooked. It was frightening. *Will I get it done in time?* I worried. *Will it taste good?* Since then I've learned that the turkeys in life take many different forms. Frankly, many things that seemed like a good idea at the time turn out to be more trouble then we ever anticipated. Few things, in fact, are ever as easy as they seem.

But I've learned a couple of others things, too. First, the really good things in life are worth the extra time and trouble. Secondly, something good can come out of even the worst situation. With God's help, our troubles really can be transformed into triumph.

Remember, too, that trials are not just for our own faith-building experience. Besides strengthening our own sense of accomplishment, they very often result in something that will feed the faith of others. Bottom line: There's always something to be thankful for.

Lord, it's not only on Thanksgiving that we find ourselves biting off more than we can chew. So many things in life become more of a challenge than we ever anticipated. Use these times to teach us patience and discipline that the end result might be a true harvest of righteousness in our lives. Amen.

CHAPTER FIVE

Tank 'Ew Much!

Give thanks in all circumstances, for this is God's will for you in Christ Jesus.
—I Thessalonians 5:18

"Tank ew much, Gamma!" For the first time my two-year-old granddaughter, Olivia, said 'thank you' without being coaxed and I did a double-take. "What did you say?" I asked, hoping for a repeat, but the moment was past. Smugly she was off, cookie in hand, to more important toddler toys and tasks.

Ever since she first started forming sentences, it had become a family effort to instill manners in this irresistible but independent child. With each cookie, drink or gift someone would quickly prompt: "What do you say?" or "Say 'thank you'"? Usually this just brought a quizzical stare from those beautiful, round, melted chocolate eyes.

Children are, after all, a bit selfish. And why not? From the time they're born someone is doing everything for them. Who wouldn't expect that kind of service to continue? No wonder any attempt at discipline is more often rewarded with a tantrum than a 'tank ew.'

Now, in one miraculous moment, the lesson had finally taken root and blossomed into an unsolicited response. Joyful tears filled my eyes. Maybe Olivia didn't understand the full scope of gratitude, but she was learning to express it anyway.

Expressing gratitude. Do any of us outgrow the need to practice until it becomes not just habit, but heartfelt? Admit it. We are all occasionally guilty of taking our loving Heavenly Father's grace for granted and acting like spoiled, ungrateful children.

I Thessalonians 5:18 reminds us it is God's will to give thanks in all circumstances. Scripture also speaks of sacrificial praise ushering us into his presence. Obviously God wants our thanks. But when we give it spontaneously? How it must truly touch His heart!

So don't even wait for Thanksgiving. "Count your blessings," says the old hymn. "Name them one by one." And should you find yourself suddenly overwhelmed by God's goodness, searching for words of gratitude—just look to heaven and holler "tank ew much!" I know Olivia would be "bery" proud.

Turning Over A New Leaf

An attitude of gratitude is something we all need to practice. *Why practice?* you say. I'm glad you asked. It's because at the very best we take a lot of God's goodness for granted. Like Olivia, if we don't get into the habit of saying thanks, we'll often forget. Then there are some things which are easier to be thankful for than others. Let's be honest, some situations come into our lives which require deep digging just to discover any nugget of good, much less gratitude. Sometimes it's simply a matter of being thankful that God is walking with us so that we don't have to go it alone.

It was during a devastating bout with breast cancer that my dear friend, Laura, started keeping a gratitude journal. Some days it was undoubtedly difficult to find many things to be thankful for. ("I didn't throw up for nearly four hours!") Yet it caused her to look for things that might have otherwise been taken for granted. Following treatment, it also provided a more positive map of the difficult journey she had just taken.

Why not start your own gratitude journal today? It's one of the best ways I know to practice an attitude of gratitude.

Lord, forgive us when we take things for granted. So many good things come from your hand and we are so often guilty of just grabbing them and running. Help us practice seeing the good in every situation until gratitude becomes an automatic part of every prayer. Amen.

CHAPTER SIX

Cross Stitch

Blessed is the man who perseveres under trial, because when he has stood the test, he will receive the crown of life that God has promised to those who love him.

—James 1:12

A few years ago at a fall retreat I bought a cross stitch kit. The display sample promised a finished product with acorns and oak leaves surrounding a simple three-word message. *How hard can that be*, the leaf lover in me whispered.

Don't count your acorns before they're stitched.

Here's how it works. Using embroidery thread you stitch horizontal rows made up of tiny crosses or 'x's. Stitch by stitch, each row must be finished before going to the next. Sounds simple, right? Sure, except with the frequent color changes, you can soon have more loose ends than a bad election ballot.

Another thing I discovered. One poorly-placed stitch requires pulling them all out and starting over. Otherwise you end up with something resembling a map of Nebraska. Unfortunately, you don't always notice this until you're a long way down the road...er, rows.

Still I was determined. Day after day I tried my best to follow the directions. Though initially I saw little resembling the final product, soon the promised picture began to materialize.

Ever feel like your life is at cross purposes? We all do our best to 'work' our lives according to God's direction, but some days we don't seem to be making much progress. Sudden changes leave us at loose ends, not to mention a few mistakes requiring 'do-overs.' Then, just as we're about to give up, it happens. A thing of beauty begins to emerge. Encouraged, we keep going. If we work it right, the end result is a life worth putting on display.

The picture now hangs in my office, its acorns and oak leaves a constant reminder of what can grow out of a small start and a persistent process.

And the three-word message? God Is Faithful. Whether through a season of change or a longer-than-we-ever-imagined process, he's with us to the last stitch.

Now here's the real beauty. Whatever happens in the middle, it all begins and ends with a single, solitary cross.

Turning Over A New Leaf

We all have them. Days when we feel like no matter how good our intentions or how hard we've tried, we made no progress at all. Worse yet, one small miscalculation has created another whole set of problems. When we finally do begin to gain momentum, some irritating interruption comes along, distracting us from our task. We know it's bad when even the days we plan to do nothing fall victim to some unscheduled setback.

Sometimes, of course, we are our own worst enemy. Wanting to hurry the process, we try to do too much, too fast. Often that's when we make mistakes and end up having to retrace our steps. We may even lose patience and want to quit, feeling like a total failure. That's the point where we may simply need to give ourselves a break, put the project aside and promise to do better tomorrow.

On the days you feel like your life is at cross purposes, here's something to remember. Nothing in God's economy is wasted. Everything we do is practice for something more important. Like anything worthwhile, the more we try, the better we get. So keep at it. Don't give up. Persevere. Keep your eyes on the cross and a beautiful pattern will eventually emerge.

Lord, life is sometimes tedious. We know you have a wonderful pattern for our lives, but sometimes we want so much to see the finished product that we lose patience in the process.

Help us remember that you know what is best and, even if it means having to rip out a few stitches, we must trust your timing. The important thing is not to give up. Point us toward the cross, Lord, and keep us going. Amen.

CHAPTER SEVEN

The Purpose Driven Quilt

For we are God's workmanship, created in Christ Jesus to do good works, which God prepared in advance for us to do.
—Ephesians 2:10

"We're so excited to have you speak for our ladies' fall retreat!" the committee chairman's voice chirped over the phone.

"My pleasure," I replied. "I've enjoyed developing your *Life With Purpose* theme."

"Oh, uh...well. That's one of the reasons I'm calling. There's been a slight change. You see, one of our committee members adores quilting, so we've decided to change our theme to *Quilts*."

QUILTS?! As she chattered on about great decorations and fun giveaways, my mind grappled to grasp some connection. *What could quilts and life with purpose possibly have in common?* Certainly nothing I'd so prayerfully and—hello!—*purposely* prepared. I'd have to change everything and the retreat was only two weeks away.

Later I none-too-kindly vented to my friend and fellow speaker, Jan. "What could these ditzy women be thinking?"

Jan chuckled. "Maybe you could just re-title your talk. Call it *The Purpose Driven Quilt*."

Very funny.

Even funnier was that I couldn't get the crazy idea out of my mind. *Crazy quilt*. Isn't that what a life without purpose can become like? Yet once committed to God, he works his plan in us, often using others in the collective process. *Collective quilt*. Each of us brings something to the table. Then, stitch by stitch, we work together until a thing of beauty begins to emerge. Something often passed to future generations. *Heirloom quilt*. The season-by-season scraps of our lives, arranged according to God's pattern, creating a legacy of warmth and wisdom for all those it touches.

The Purpose-Driven Quilt. Who'd a thought?

Now only one thing remained ...

Forgive me, Lord, for this crazy quilt crisis. Thanks for using these great gals (oh, and sorry about that 'ditzy' remark!) to smooth out a few of my own wrinkles. We truly are your workmanship—once we get out of the way and give you elbow room. Now please weave these pieces together for our good and your glory. Amen.

Amazing, isn't it, what God does? On purpose.

Turning Over A New Leaf

Anyone besides me remember what were once called 'quilting bees'? These were gatherings much like the scrapbooking parties that are so popular today, but instead of pictures and keepsakes, women from the church or community brought scraps of fabric. Then stitch by stitch, they worked together toward the common goal of constructing a beautiful and colorful quilted blanket such as the ones often seen hanging in someone's house or an antique store.

What a bonding experience it must have been. Undoubtedly a lot of life-pieces got sorted out and pieced together over those quilting tables as well. These were times that provided fellowship and instruction, while still resulting in a service to those who benefitted from the final product.

Most often it was the older women who taught the younger. Ever stop to think that none of us would have any wisdom or knowledge if someone hadn't taken the time to teach us? Not a bad thing to remember when we're tempted to expect too much from others or from ourselves for that matter.

Lord, thank you for working the pieces of our lives together. Collectively we can accomplish so much more than any one of us can do alone. Help us to keep working on the pattern you have planned so that the end result might be a thing of beauty, a legacy worth leaving. Amen.

CHAPTER EIGHT

Fringe Benefits

But grow in the grace and knowledge of our Lord and Saviour Jesus Christ. To him be glory both now and forever. Amen.
—II Peter 3:18

One major misconception many of us have is that once we mature we'll have a better handle on keeping our lives in balance. I wish someone would tell me at what magical age that happens. Seems the older I get, the more responsibilities I have and the more realistically I'm forced to look at life. I hate it when that happens. Evidently so did architect Frank Lloyd Wright who said, "The trick is to grow up without getting old." I wholeheartedly agree.

Truth is, sometimes I embarrass my kids and grandkids with my silly, spontaneous actions. Take for instance a jacket I recently ordered from a catalog—light brown suede with long fringe hanging from the sleeves and yoke, sort of like something the historic sharpshooter Annie Oakley might have worn. I'd wanted one of those jackets ever since I was nine years old.

Surprisingly, when I pointed it out to my much more conservative husband, he said "Go for it." Maybe he's lightening up a little in his old age, too. So I did. It's hard to explain how putting on that jacket makes me feel—frivolous, lighthearted and, yes, years younger.

Of course, we've all known people who, in an attempt to abate the aging process, have done some really weird and wacky things. The balance we need to heed is recorded in II Peter 3:18: "But grow in the grace and knowledge of our Lord and Savior, Jesus Christ. To him be glory both now and forever! Amen." That's the key: to be sure that the older we get, the more our lives bring him glory.

The reality is that growing up does often dictate the demise of a few youthful fantasies, but it doesn't have to mean the death of your dreams. There's a difference. And if you're able to reclaim a fun fantasy or two along the way, well, that's what I'd call one of the fringe benefits.

Turning Over A New Leaf

One of the exciting things about changing seasons is that though the Lord often closes one door, he always opens another. For as long as I can remember, I have had a love affair with words and writing. For years my greatest creative endeavor was an annual newsletter, mailed to family and friends who often responded with kindness and encouragement. Though at the time I had no serious ambitions about ever being published, turns out two of my first published pieces were ones written during these years.

Looking back now I can see how God was leading me in the direction of my gifting, even providing me with basic grammar and composition training. Still, it would be years before the opportunity for publication was presented. Why? Because the Lord knew I still had some growing to do, both in grace and knowledge, so that when he finally released me to pursue my passion for writing, it would be for his glory, not my own.

Do you have a dream? Keep learning and growing. Embrace the experiences that God brings your way. Who, but he, knows what exciting opportunities the next season in your life will bring?

Lord, your Word tells us to delight ourselves in you and you will give us the desires of our hearts. Help us to keep that in proper perspective, knowing that as we seek to serve you, you will cause us to grow in the areas of our best and most effective gift. Then we can rest assured that it will always be not only for our good but, most important, for your glory. Amen.

CHAPTER NINE

As Time Goes By

Only be careful and watch yourself closely so that you do not forget the things your eyes have seen or let them slip from your heart as long as you live. Teach them to your children and to their children after them.
—Deuteronomy 4:9

The streets of Old Folsom were vibrant with the colors and shapes of autumn. Corn stalks, pumpkins, and every variety of mum and marigold decorated the median on Main Street, casting an earth-toned rainbow of orange, yellow, rust and bronze against the century-old buildings.

One could almost wonder in the afternoon glow if daylight savings time had caused this place to fall back years rather than just an hour. The theme was duplicated in each specialty shop display window as I wandered casually down the wooden sidewalk savoring the combined atmosphere of California harvest and history.

When I reached a favorite shop whose name, "As Time Goes By", fit my mood of seasonal reflection, I turned in. Though immediately enveloped by the luring fragrance of spice-scented candles, I couldn't help but notice a father, carrying a toddler, navigate two preschool daughters deftly around the displays that would usually tempt youngsters. Heading straight to a corner brightly stocked with items for children, they were obviously on a mission. Absently I smiled and resumed my browsing.

A few minutes later, as I was paying for the two items I had been unable to resist, they approached the register.

"Excuse me," the young father addressed the proprietor. "Do you have Peking, the panda bear?" I glanced at the two preschoolers at his side who waited for the answer with large expectant eyes.

"I'm sorry," she answered, "if there are none on the shelf we must have sold the last one." Then she added, half to him, half to me, "Boy, those went fast!"

It was just then that I noticed two small pandas on a display wall behind the counter and asked if those could be the ones they were looking for.

A bright look crossed the faces, then disappointment. "No," came a small lisping voice, "the oneths we want are Beanie Babies—thoseth are not the thame."

Beanie Babies were the latest infatuation for young collectors. Immediately I understood, and my mind replayed a similar scene from twenty years ago, only the roles were reversed. This time as a young mother I walked down the aisle of a large toy store, carrying my three-year old son with two other small boys in tow.

It was the fourth store we'd been to and it, too, was completely sold out of Jawas—the latest, just-released action figure from the *Star Wars* movie. Hundreds of other action figures hung on display, but they weren't the "thame."

What we choose to collect most certainly tells something about each young generation's times and trends. For me, and every other kid growing up in the fifties, it was cowboys, Indians and horses. I can remember my mother and me going from store to store to find a porcelain horse that was different from the rest of my collection.

I have come to understand over the years that part of the joy of collecting—be it Beanie Babies, action figures, or horses—often has as much to do with the finding as it does with the having. Though it may be that acquiring every new collectible is the most important quest at the time, the childhood memories that are ultimately connected to those things will only come into proper perspective as experience presses us into adulthood.

Each porcelain horse riding on the white clouds of a Kansas summer afternoon allowed a child to believe that someday she'd have a horse of her very own, encouraging imagination. Each molded and painted action figure reminded a boy of an afternoon *Star Wars* matinee with his dad. And perhaps a floppy, furry friend filled with beans will eventually evoke a memory of the golden autumn day in Old Folsom when a father and his daughters went to just one more store looking for that special panda to add to the collection of other Beanies.

As I turned to leave the shop I heard the young father say that they would just have to look someplace else. Stepping out into the lengthening rays of the autumn afternoon, my eyes fell again on the shop's signature plate, "As Time Goes By." Not only were the days getting shorter, so was the time. I thought of my own grandchildren. There had to be a shop nearby where I could find those pandas for their collection of Beanie Babies. And memories.

> *If the world seems cold to you,*
> *kindle fires to warm it.*
> —Author Unknown

WINTER

Winter blows in on a chilly but cheerful wind of holiday planning and anticipation, snow flurries often mixing with the flurry of activities. From Santas to snowflakes to stars, the signs of the season are everywhere. Store windows, houses and yards twinkle with every type of traditional trapping. Carols come at us from all electronic angles. Parties are planned and people deplane as families gather from near and far to celebrate. Christmas truly is the most wonderful time of the year.

Then it's over.

The wrappings and trappings are trashed and stashed and we find ourselves facing the reality that another entire year has passed. The time has now come for reflection and resolutions. Where did the time go? What did we do with it? Suddenly a clean calendar looms before us. What improvements can we make in the coming year? Facing the stark stretch of remaining winter months, there's certainly no cause to rush the contemplation. Now comes the true time of waiting and wishing—waiting for the dark days and cold temperatures to end, wishing for longer light and warmer climates.

At some point, spiritually speaking, we will all face winter seasons as well. It's not unusual for them to hit hard on the heels of what has seemed a much more exhilarating and productive time in our lives. Like the cold draft from an opened door, the warmth seems suddenly sucked from our souls and we find ourselves asking, "What happened to the season of celebration, Lord?" or, "Now what?" and even, "Why?" It's then we may find ourselves waiting in the cold silence and wondering if we will ever again feel the sun's warmth and the stirrings of life.

Perhaps the reason a good number of people get depressed during the holidays is that they focus too much on the commercial and not enough on the spiritual. Even in the starkness of winter there is amazing beauty, if we will take the time to look for it—the serenity of snowy silence or clarity of bare branches against a flaming winter sunset. We need these times of contrast, of waiting and wondering, of introspection and insulation, to put our lives into perspective. Like the seed buried beneath the snow, sometimes this is the time that the deepest work in our lives is being done, though we may not see it until a later season. The important thing during any time of seeming spiritual isolation is that we don't despair. Psychologists tell us never to make a major life decision when we're depressed. Likewise, we need to wait out the spiritual winters of our lives, feeding on the comfort food found in God's word. Consider a familiar phrase in scripture: "And it came to pass." This season will, too.

To help you pass the time, here are some stories illustrating warm spiritual lessons during a cold season of waiting.

CHAPTER ONE

Head Start on the Holidays

After Jesus was born in Bethlehem... Magi came from the east to Jerusalem and asked, "Where is the one who has been born king of the Jews?"
—Matthew 2:1

When the first Christmas catalog arrived in August, I determined to get a head start on holiday gift-buying. First, however, I had to get in the mood. Cranking the air conditioner down to 48 degrees, I donned my favorite cedar-scented reindeer sweater, popped in a Christmas CD and brewed a cup of hot cocoa. An hour later my husband found me passed out in a puddle of perspiration, the catalog stuck on my face with half-melted miniature marshmallows.

"What in the world are you doing?" he asked, shaking me awake.

"Gotta get an early start...Christmas is coming," I mumbled.

Amused consternation crossed his face. "Christmas is four months away. Besides, honey, buying early doesn't work for you. Remember?"

He was right.

Take the year I decided to hit the after-Christmas sales and buy our three boys clothes for the following Christmas. That was also the year they all took unbelievable growth spurts. As a result, the youngest kid made out like a bandit while the others went naked until the stores re-opened on December 26th.

Besides, if I buy early, it's a miracle if I'm able to wait until the holiday to give them their gifts. The suspense is just too much for me. Sure, I've tried stashing the stuff so I wouldn't be tempted, only to forget about it completely—which explains the snowman socks in my grandchildren's Easter baskets.

Then there's the matter of Christmas cards. Undaunted by fastidious friends who mail theirs to arrive annually on December 1st, I finally decided a New Year letter works best into my schedule. Anytime in the first quarter qualifies, right?

My only consolation is that the original Christmas gift-givers weren't exactly ahead of the game either. Contrary to the common depiction of the wise men around the manger, Matthew's gospel makes it clear they were actually two years tardy—despite astrological ads and a big head start. So what made them so wise? I guess it was the fact that they at least had the good sense to bring gifts that didn't spoil, need batteries or have to be returned.

Turning Over A New Leaf

Every year we tell ourselves the same thing. We'll get it all done early this year and actually enjoy the holiday. No more waiting until the last minute to buy gifts, bake cookies and bedeck the banisters.

For those of you who actually get ahead of the game and stay there, more power to you. I've come to the conclusion that getting a head start on the holidays may actually be hazardous to my health, but not for the somewhat exaggerated examples above.

The big problem for me, I realized long ago, was my own unrealistic expectations. My craving for a Christmas card perfect holiday was causing me—and everyone else—to stress out, not only losing the spirit but often forgetting the focus.

Want a real head start on the holidays? Let a word from the wise men be sufficient. "Where is he that is born King of the Jews?" they asked. An honest answer to that question should give us all a true head start, not just on the holidays but the whole year.

Lord, it's your birthday. Yet it's so easy for us to fall into the trappings trap. Forgive us. Help us to put you first, not only in our celebration but in our souls. We'll be wise, too, if only we'll remember that you truly are the reason for the season and plan everything else accordingly. Amen.

CHAPTER TWO

Being Truly Gifted

Thanks be to God for his indescribable gift!
—II Corinthians 9:15

When it comes to selecting spousal Christmas gifts, we have made ...well, let's just say...a few errors in judgment over the years.

By his own admission, my husband is not the most creative gift-giver. Twice, early on, he even resorted to soliciting help from my friends. The first try turned up an outfit that perfectly suited the svelte sidekick who chose it but in which I resembled a stuffed sausage. The second—an attempt at surprise—employed two buddies best known for their not-so-practical pranks. Inside a beautiful box lay earrings that could've doubled as belt buckles and a vase I couldn't unload in a garage sale. It was a surprise, all right.

For my part, there was that unfortunate knitting phase. But we won't go there.

Since then we've managed to keep the holiday spirit intact by establishing a few basic rules: Appliances are not romantic. Returning a gift does not constitute personal rejection. If you can't be creative, at least be adept at taking hints. Bigger doesn't equal better. And, yes, there is a vast difference between Godiva and Hickory Farms.

The kids and grandkids take no risks. First, they explain exactly what they want, where to find it and how much it costs. Then they sucker us with sentiment. For instance, when recently asked what he was getting for Christmas, our grandson boldly blurted the name of the most recent, red-hot video game.

"How can you be sure?" his dad asked.

"Cuz I told Grampa and he *always* gets me what I want."

Who could burst that bubble? Even if it means scouring several stores, risking personal injury wrestling the last one off the shelf, then standing in a check-out line that extends into the next county.

There can be only one reason why we put ourselves through this annual angst. Insanity? No. Love.

And we're in good company.

"For God so loved the world that He gave his only begotten Son…"

Talk about the Perfect Gift.

Turning Over A New Leaf

No doubt about it. Picking out the perfect gift can be tricky. Every year we find ourselves agonizing over the same querulous quandaries. What can we get that he or she doesn't already have? Should we buy something useful or frivolous? How can we be creative, yet cost conscious? Will they like this color and style? In frustration, many of us less courageous souls finally resort to what seems safest: gift certificates, gourmet goodies or hard, cold cash.

Amazing, when we love someone, the lengths we'll go to in procuring something that promises to please. In the end, that's what makes it really special. Whether it's the macaroni beads our kindergartner made in school or the diamond earrings we've been hinting about for months, the fact that someone loved us enough to make or choose it especially for us far overshadows the monetary value, not to mention any minor (or major) misjudgments.

Certainly God showed us by his own example. Anytime we give love, we've given the perfect gift.

Lord, thank you for loving us enough to give the perfect gift—your Son. May we, too, along with whatever gift we choose, be sure that it's always generously wrapped it in love. Amen.

CHAPTER THREE

The Best Laid Plans

In his heart a man plans his course, But the Lord determines his steps.
—Proverbs 16:9

Holiday plans. We all have them. Plans to host the annual family dinner, emulate magazine-perfect decorations, make every gift, escape for a ski weekend. Why is it, then, that our best laid plans don't always materialize? I can sum it up in one word: Interruptions. Defined "inter-" (in the middle of something) "ruptions" (kaboom!) Something happens and that synchronized celebration unravels like Aunt Erma's hand-knit afghan.

Still we refuse to make allowances. Interruptions simply do not fit in our plan; otherwise they'd be called intentions. Instead we proceed in a fudge-induced frenzy, determined to make merry memories no matter who it kills. No wonder, then, the inevitable disruptions are viewed as frustrations, rarely blessings.

I beg you. Stop now. Step away from your preposterous, self-imposed schedule and no one will get hurt. Consider a lesson from my young friend, Trevor.

At a large gathering of Trevor's family, the adults—busy visiting and cooking—had left the youngsters to devise their own entertainment. This predictably escalated into a mad chase through the house. Just as things reached the point of requiring adult intervention, Trevor suddenly raced in. "I'm outta control," he announced. "I'm giving myself a time out!" And plopped down in the middle of the floor to do just that.

Ah, for Trevor's wisdom. But we are responsible adults, right? We know when we're racing around haphazardly and need to slow down.

Right.

Maybe that's why God, like any good parent, often has to do it for us. Hence, the interruptions.

Solomon, with Trevor-like wisdom, wrote: "In his heart a man plans his course, but the Lord determines His steps." (Proverbs 16:9). Could it be that while I am barreling down the holiday highway fullspeed, God is planning some designated detours?

I imagine the shepherds had their agenda on that starry night in Bethlehem just before God's Son eternally interrupted history's plans. It took angels to get their attention, but didn't it create a memorable holiday?

Turning Over A New Leaf

On the days when nothing seems to go as we planned, have you ever considered that interruptions might actually be part of a greater plan—God's plan? Most of us have heard the familiar saying, "The best laid plans of mice and men often go astray." The good news is God cares for mice and men. Both are his creations, but mankind is the one He loved enough to make in His own image, with the map to eternity hand-drawn on his heart. No wonder it is important to God that we not get too far off the path.

While the occasional major interruption may come to bring—or yank!—us back on the path of reality, many serve merely to capture our diverted attention, contribute to developing patience, halt us long enough to get our bearings, or provide an opportunity to minister into someone else's interrupted life.

Some are serendipitous surprises. For there are also those times when God intervenes to bless us in ways we never hoped or imagined. I'd say that's something worth being interrupted for. Wouldn't you agree?

Lord, how many times do we make plans without even asking your direction? Then we get upset when things don't work out the way we wanted them to. Help us commit our way to you and trust you to bring it to pass. That way whatever happens, we'll know your hand is in it. Amen.

CHAPTER FOUR

Why Am I Doing This?

Let us not become weary in doing good, for at the proper time we will keep a harvest if we do not give up.

—Galatians 6:9

"Why am I doing this?" It's the inevitable question of every busy holiday season.

As a pastor's wife for 25 years, I organized more major productions than Steven Spielberg. I still see myself sitting at the sewing machine, up to my eyeglasses in costumes or puppets. Directing a struggling choir with too many altos but never enough tenors. Assembling stage sets until the wee small hours. Baking, cooking and cleaning for our annual open house. Stretching an already transparent budget. Wondering if things will ever come together, why I push my limits and whether it is worth all the trouble anyhow. In exhausted frustration, the question finally explodes. "Why am I doing this?!"

Now as District officials, we no longer serve just one congregation. And of all things, I miss the church's holiday programs the most. Go figure.

OK, maybe not the exhausting preparations—admittedly, it's hard work. But I do miss experiencing the intangible rewards: warm feelings of accomplishment, satisfaction and, of course, the ultimate relief.

From my scrapbook of pastoral memories come random snapshots. Churches so small there was no one but us to plan and produce. An adorable round-faced Alaskan child who never before played a shepherd. The huge fireplace in a snow-encrusted log cabin flickering warmly on an all-church Thanksgiving dinner. The miracle of a children's musical performed two weeks after the previous director up and quit. Sanctuaries, large and small, filled with seasonal sounds and scents. Patriotic pageants reinforcing our Godly heritage.

Snuggling on the couch with my pastor-husband in the post-open-house quiet amid scattered plates and leftovers. Shoes kicked off, holding hands. Wondering where we'd find the strength to clean up, yet basking in the glow of seeing our congregation woven together with lasting friendships.

Sitting in a candlelight service with my children, the sweet assurance and restoring presence of the Lord filling that place. Feeling the cozy blanket of beloved believers wrapped around me.

"Why am I doing this?" Oh, I think you know.

Turning Over A New Leaf

No doubt about it. The holidays can be hectic. It's easy for us to get so caught up in the preparations that we completely lose perspective, not to mention end up just plain pooped. Is it worth it? It is if lives are touched and hearts turned toward the Savior, whose birth we celebrate.

After all, it is the one time of year when peace and good will are in a little larger supply, often providing more opportunity for sharing and caring than we may find at other times.

So go ahead. Bake another batch of cookies and toss a tad more tinsel. Even if you go a bit overboard, you have a whole year to rest up. The hope is that you'll be able to look back over your own personal scrapbook revealing the memorable, meaningful moments behind the madness. May the love you show and the memories you make stay in the hearts of those you touch for years to come.

Lord, thank you again for coming. Emanuel—God with us. Because you came we have joy, hope and peace. Help us to share that with all those we come in contact with during this special season. All year around, may all we do bring glory to God in the highest, peace on earth, good will toward men. Amen.

CHAPTER FIVE

After the Holidays, the Rest Is Gravy

May your unfailing love be my comfort,
according to your promise to your servant.
—Psalm 119:76

When the going gets tough...the tough make pot pie. That's my theory and I'm sticking to it. Thus, I found myself welcoming the New Year up to my elbows in biscuit dough and gravy.

Our whole clan came for Christmas—a wonderful week of food, laughter, lights and the magical music box of children's voices. Hectic, yes, but happy. Then they were gone and the house was blessedly quiet. Too bloomin', blessedly quiet!

I tried to pick up where I'd left off...after I picked up what they had left. But every forgotten stinky sock, hair twisty, and hidden bit of wrapping brought a familiar freckle-faced memory. Sigh.

Then I noticed something else. We received no complimentary New Year calendars. You know, the ones organizations send featuring seasonal settings with sappy inscriptions. Usually we are deluged with them. Of course I had my five-year day-timer, which was...oh dear...now six years old.

For two weeks I stared at December, realizing that time had moved on without me. I was stuck between Merry Christmas and Empty New Year.

Empty? Say, maybe I was just hungry.

That's when I found myself preparing chicken pot pie—my mother's rendition, combining leftovers, fresh ingredients and love to produce something sustaining and good. Not unlike life, really.

As the mixture bubbled, I hummed, grateful for the unexplainable comfort produced by combining faith in something tested with a daily routine. Suddenly it hit me: faith in God's tested faithfulness as we go about our daily routine. Isn't that, inevitably, the 'gravy' that holds us together? Suddenly I felt full.

Next I'll buy a calendar; but I'll add my own inscription, thank you! Yet I am not ashamed (have no regrets), because I know whom I have believed, and am convinced that he is able to guard what I have entrusted to him for that day (II Timothy 1:12b). It's my life verse, but I'll let you borrow it this year.

Now go make a pot pie.

Turning Over A New Leaf

Amazing, isn't it, how many of our best memories revolve around food. Certainly every family has their favorite special meals. While chicken pot pie is still one of mine, there's nothing that will bring our own grown sons running like biscuits and gravy for breakfast or the traditional Braddy birthday lasagna. Why is food so important? Because making favorite meals is one of the ways we show our love.

Obviously, though, it goes beyond just good eating. These are time-tested recipes—often passed, with minor variations, from one generation to the next—guaranteed to turn out the same way every time. Something we can depend on. That, along with the attached memories of warm kitchens and families gathered around the table, is the real reason they call it comfort food. No matter how families grow, or where they go, these recipes stick not only to the ribs, but to the heart.

Someday, Scripture tells us, we will all be gathered together for the marriage supper of the Lamb, never to be parted again. Just thinking of that is the best recipe I know for beating the after-the-holiday blues.

Lord, you are our comfort and our strength, a very present help in time of trouble. Feed us with your word. May we be sustained not only by memories of the past, but the hope you give us for the future. Just knowing that you are faithful and can be trusted is all the comfort we need. Amen.

CHAPTER SIX

Losers, Take Heart!

I press on toward the goal to win the prize for which God has called me heavenward in Christ Jesus.
—Philippians 3:14

Click. Whir. ZZZiippp. Silence. "Aaarrgh!"

The bathroom scale blinked apologetically, confirming my suspicion. A caravan of calories had hitched a ride into the New Year. The holidays were now, quite literally, *behind* me.

The next morning found me outside the neighborhood women's workout center where a sign read: "Amaze yourself!" Nervously putting one Nike in front of the other, I stepped in. It *was* amazing! Women of every size, age and ethnicity circled the room, bouncing and puffing from one exercise station to another. High-energy music whirled them like a bionic blender.

Winter

I took a deep, spandex-scented breath. OK. I could do this. Only a few jogs and jiggles to a new me. Piece-a-cake...er, celery. Think thin, think thin...

Before you could say carbohydrate, I was weighed, measured and maneuvered feet-first into my new circle of sole sisters. I'd just tripped onto the bounce board when a tape-recorded voice purred, "Move to the next machine." As I debated which direction, the sister on my right spring-boarded me to the left. My arms were barely wedged into the next contraption when the voice cooed again. This time I moved quickly...well, most of me. Halfway to the next station my still-wedged arm yelped, "Hold it!"

Soon, tingly arm notwithstanding, I was progressing productively.

"Now step away from your machine." Finally, a voice of reason. Simultaneously everyone saluted a lady in an American flag T-shirt. *Strange time for the pledge of allegiance*, I thought. Oh, we were checking heart rates. Mine was still doing the conga.

Three cycles and a cool-down later, schlepping toward the exit, I noticed another sign:

"Prizes for the top three losers." Losers can be winners?! Somehow I found that not only encouraging, but scriptural.

"Not that I have already obtained...or have already been made perfect..." Paul writes to the Philippians, "but I press on to take hold of that for which Christ Jesus took hold of me." Seems losing whatever weighs us down, physically or spiritually, comes only with patient perseverance. But the eternal reward is incomparable. A big ole' non-fattening piece of Heavenly pie!

Turning Over A New Leaf

Amazing how things can creep up on you, both physically and spiritually. Physically it starts with an extra piece of pie here, a cookie there and before you know it, you're carrying around more than just the empty cardboard containers. One step on the scale or look in the mirror and there goes self-esteem, right out the window. *How could I have let this happen?* we wonder, knowing that the weight's going to be a lot harder to take off than it was to put on.

Spiritually it's just the opposite. It's not what we take in, but what we put off. It starts by missing one day of daily devotions. Then two. Before we know it, we've allowed anything and everything to interfere with our vital daily visit with the Lord. Soon not only are we completely out of the habit of reading God's word, but our prayer life has gotten pretty puny as well. This leaves plenty of room for the accuser to come in. "You have no discipline at all," he sneers. "You're just a big loser."

So what's a loser to do? Get back with the program, of course. Press on. Knowing Jesus is already at the finish line, cheering us on and holding out the prize.

Lord, in ourselves we are weak, imperfect and undisciplined. We need your strength every single day. Help us remember that the prize is already won—we just have to claim it. As far as you're concerned, we're already winners. Amen.

CHAPTER SEVEN

Photo Opportunity

Aim for perfection...and the God of love and peace will be with you.
—II Corinthians 13:11

How would our recent holiday pictures turn out? My husband, Jim, and I sat at the kitchen table, ripping into a stack of envelopes from the local photo department. We could hardly wait to see.

"Look," I chirped. "Here are all the kids gathered around the Christmas barbeque, holding their new sparklers." *Barbeque...sparklers!?* "Good grief, these are from last Fourth of July."

"Farther back than that," Jim says, chuckling at the batch he holds, "unless you gave them Easter baskets for Christmas."

I've been exposed. When it comes to producing timely pictures, I am developmentally challenged.

That's if I even remember my camera. According to Jim, all the disposable cameras I buy are what keep Kodak in business. Not to mention the quantity of film. Can I help it if there's always a better shot around the corner? Or that every subject seems equally fascinating from eight different angles?

No doubt the money spent could have financed one of those fancy new digital cameras—the kind allowing you to do-over, then print only the pictures you like. I'm told that once downloaded, even flaws can even be digitally deleted.

Truth is, though, I prefer the pictures that show life as it really happens. Like the kid with a finger up their nose, grandma's unflattering but hilarious expression, or the south end of an animal that suddenly turned north.

They serve to remind us that life offers no guarantee the picture we want is the one we'll actually get. Believe me, the more people involved, the less likely it will be perfect. Still, it's sure to be interesting, which is not necessarily a negative.

By the time we found the Christmas pictures, we'd reminisced through a whole year's glossy gallery of events. It was amazing what had transpired.

Sometimes we "shutter" to think what an entire new year holds. Perhaps we need to reframe our expectations. "Aim for perfection," Paul instructs, then leaves us with this encouragement. "And the God of love and peace will be with you."

Picture that. Not only does God already know what will develop, he's standing in the center of every single snapshot.

Turning Over A New Leaf

No doubt about it, a year can pass quickly and it's always amazing to look back and see all that transpired. Sometimes, after the fact, it can be a bit scary. That's why it's best that we take life one frame at a time. Some things, I'm convinced, we would not want to know ahead of time.

This was something that took on a very personal significance for my husband, Jim, and I recently when, on the last night of a visit from all our kids and grandkids, he suddenly began experiencing severe chest pains. A mad dash to the emergency room followed by a battery of tests revealed the need for five-way coronary bypass surgery—something which, with absolutely no previous symptoms, came as a complete surprise.

In retrospect we realize how gracious God was in protecting him and allowing us to discover his heart condition when and how we did. Only a week before, we had taken our the whole gang to a local amusement park and Jim had ridden one of those crazy new rollercoasters. What if his heart had acted up then?

Through it all I can tell you this. God was there, loving us and giving us his peace. Whatever the outcome, whether positive or negative, we had the assurance that his plan would always involve a great photo finish.

> *Lord, whatever the days, months and years of our lives hold, they are in your hands. You alone see the big picture. We'll do our best to always aim for perfection, but should life turn out less than what we expected, help us continue to trust you frame by frame. Amen.*

CHAPTER EIGHT

A Pearl of Wisdom

I thank my God every time I remember you.
—Philippians 1:3

She wore her gray hair twisted into a bun at the base of her neck, just low enough to show under the stylish hats popular in the 1950's. We never knew her age, just that she was really old—59, at least. But what did it matter? Every week she told us stories about Jesus. And on our birthdays, everyone got invited to her house for a Sunday afternoon party complete with fried chicken and chocolate cake. Her love for the Lord and for us was so real. We knew her simply as Sister Jarvis, our fourth grade Sunday school teacher and, for that year at least, our very best friend.

Make no mistake, though. Graduating from her class didn't mean Sister Jarvis stopped caring. Forever after she took a special interest in "her girls." No surprise, then, that a few years later near Christmas she poked a large envelope into my hand. She'd heard I was taking piano lessons and wanted me to have a coveted piece of her own sheet music—a seasonal selection entitled *Put Christ Back Into Christmas*. But not before she imparted just one more lesson. "Christmas is getting too commercial, Judi. Let's keep reminding folks of the real meaning."

Placing the music on my piano stand later that day, I recognized her bold script on the upper right corner: Esther Pearl Jarvis. It was the first time I knew she had three names.

Sister Jarvis taught Sunday school for many more years, then lived independently well into her nineties. Long after I'd gone away to college and married my minister husband. And though I've had many wonderful mentors over the years, it's amazing how those early lessons from Esther Pearl have remained the simplest yet truest fundamentals of my life and ministry. Love the Lord. Love others. And keep reminding people what's most important

Truly, they are pearls of wisdom worthy of passing on. Just like Sister Jarvis.

Turning Over A New Leaf

What can possibly be better than a clean load of softly scented laundry that has just come out of the dryer? Something about the warmth and aroma begs us to bury ourselves in it. True confession: I've been known to do just that. Especially if it's a cushy comforter, a warm woven blanket or a plush pair of socks on a cold winter's day.

This is how I like to think of the wonderful women God has brought into my life over the years to soften and sweeten my load. Not to mention conserve the color. Undoubtedly many have provided a blanket of warmth and comfort when the world around me seemed cold, unfair and unforgiving.

Haven't we all had them—friends, teachers and relatives, anyone who provided positive input and brought balance? Surely, if we take the time, each of us can recall at least one mentor for every milestone. Some have short-term influence, some long-term, but all leave a bit of themselves with us. And we are softer, sweeter people because of them.

> *We're thankful, Lord, each time we think of the many friends and mentors you've blessed our lives with. We need all the support, encouragement and influence we can get. Give us the grace, as well, even as we're piecing our own lives together, to contribute to the pattern in others. Amen.*

CHAPTER NINE

Bah, Flu Bug!

"But we have this treasure in jars of clay..."
—II Corinthians 4:7

'Tis the week after Christmas and all through the house, the only thing stirring is me and my mouse. Never mind that it's now 3:45 a.m. My computer screen casts a querulous glow, not quite ready to work. I know the feeling.

Recovering from a recent flu bug, my cough alarm has "rung" at 3 a.m. for the last three days. Experience has taught me there is no snooze button, so in preference to others sleeping, I stumble downstairs to put the kettle on, dressed in the haute couture of illness—my husband's plaid flannel robe, a t-shirt, sweat pants, and my fake leopard slippers. I would also be wearing his old wool athletic socks if he hadn't callously thrown them away at some point, obviously not realizing their significance in the flu recovery process.

One never really embraces sickness, but more concedes to it running its course. First, there is the initial denial. "Are you getting sick?" someone asks as you clear your throat for the thirtieth time in a minute. "No," you answer quickly, horrified that someone would speak the very words you've been thinking. "It's probably just allergies or sinus drainage." Well, of course it's sinus drainage, silly person. That's what happens what you get sick.

You carry on valiantly, sure that you can beat this thing. Finally one morning you awake, aching and feverish, realizing too late that death is surely only moments away and you should have done more for the poor and needy. You have lost the battle.

What follows are three or four delirious days and equal gallons of chicken soup. If you're fortunate like me, someone will eventually notice that you haven't moved and ask if they can get you anything. Don't get me wrong. My family is loving and considerate, just a little preoccupied. Also this usually coincides with the day when there is nothing left in the kitchen that can be heated in the microwave.

By this time, though, you know you must be getting better because everything that has caused your head to expand three sizes is suddenly, uncontrollably released. Ironically, you are also out of tissue.

By the grace of God and a roll of toilet paper, you survive and have another shot at helping the helpless. When you are finally able to focus on your surroundings, it becomes immediately apparent who they are. Caution: take this last step slowly as it has been known to cause an immediate relapse in those of weaker constitution.

To my surprise, shortly after that pivotal moment of hanging between life and death, an unusual sense of clarity seemed to present itself. So I awoke this morning, blessedly clear-headed, without the fuzzy edges, feeling I could once again risk assuming a future. That's when I turned on my computer and cautiously stepped back into the land of the productive, trusting that whatever came out would be tempered by the great lessons I learned from this season of sickness.

"What are those lessons?" you ask. They are: To be reminded again how fragile and precious life is and that there are no real guarantees. That everything can change in a day, an hour or even a minute. At best, we all live with a limited warranty so it is important to make the most of the time we have with family and friends. Finally, to always acknowledge, thankfully, God's faithfulness in every area of our lives.

Perhaps there is no better time to be reminded of all these things than in the aftermath of the holidays when life can be so stressful and out of control.

So, am I glad I got the flu? No. Am I glad it was just the flu? You bet your vitamin C! Truth is, starting the New Year with the right perspective just might have been worth getting a flu bug for Christmas.

Winter's done, and April's in the skies;
Earth, look up with laughter in your eyes.
—John Masefield

SPRING

Spring comes every year, yet it always surprises me, perhaps because it seems to happen so quickly. One day it's cold and drizzly—the next everything seems to be blooming.

Of course the signs are there long before. Take buds, for instance. *Honestly*, I found myself thinking one cold, foggy February morning when I first noticed them, *don't those buds know it's still winter?* I even attempted a warning: "Don't come out! It's too early…you'll freeze!" Obviously, though, the trees know something I don't. Somewhere in their roots the rising sap sends secret signals. The shiny brown bumps patiently await their moment of release. Then, with the sun's first warmth, they burst like pink and white popcorn. And the show begins. I'm quite certain I even heard several tiny "ta-das"!

Simple Seasons

Following the stark, soggy winter, spring seems optimistically opulent. Plants overflow with flowers. Rolling hills get new green carpet, some with serendipitous stripes of color as wild flowers spring from seeds sown randomly by winter's winds. Leaves tenderly unfold, shimmering on branches like ethereal emeralds.

Little creatures come curiously out of hiding. Soon everywhere something is jumping or flitting. Nighttime brings a cacophony of choruses. Every morning the still-distant sun reflects spring's vibrant colors in diamonds of dew.

Goodness. It's downright bright and noisy out there! The world comes once again to life, and God just can't keep it to Himself. Aren't you glad?

For emotions, too, run the seasonal gamut. We all love life's easy-growing summer seasons, chafe at the changes of autumn's inevitable transitions, and shiver when winter blows its dark despondency across our souls.

Then unfailingly it happens. At some point in every chilly, cheerless winter, the Creator's "sap" sends secret signals. Buds of hope appear and ultimately in the Son's warmth, something full of beauty, hope and promise begins to burst forth.

If you listen closely, you may even hear a tiny, angelic "ta-da!"

Spiritually speaking, in the midst of any long, cold season, it's often hard to believe that spring will ever come. But it always does. You arise one morning and suddenly sense it: God is doing something new and fresh.

Solomon pens it perfectly in his Song of Songs: *See! the winter is past; the rains are over and gone. Flowers appear on the earth; the season of singing has come, the cooing of doves is heard in our land. The fig tree forms its early fruit; the blossoming vines spread their fragrance. Arise, come, my darling; my beautiful one, come with me.* (Song of Solomon 2:11-13)

So, arise, my darling, and read. The stories in this section illustrate spiritual lessons in the most renewing, hopeful and promising season of all.

CHAPTER ONE

Growing By Leaps and Bounds

So neither he who plants nor he who waters is anything, but only God, who makes things grow.
—I Corinthians 3:7

To be a gardener, you really only have to have one thing: faith. Faith to believe that the seeds you placed so hopefully in the chilly spring soil will soon be full-grown plants. That in return for the proper care, they should soon start paying you back with fabulous flowers or fruit. Fact is, if past experience is any teacher, it doesn't take all that much faith to know that if you plant zucchini, you'll eventually be looking for people to give it to—perhaps even resorting to anonymously leaving them on stranger's doorsteps or in their cars.

Most people consider gardening a seasonal hobby, but serious gardeners know that preparation for the growing season takes place all year around.

Spring

After the final summer harvest, the spent vines must be discarded and the soil turned. During the cold months perennials must be protected, even as plans are made for the next season's crop. While they wait, gardeners discuss pests and problems, even exchange seeds. Then, awaiting the final frost, they incubate the seeds inside until, finally, the sun warms the soil and it's time to plant.

It's then they may even discover a "volunteer" plant or two—latent seeds that sprout unexpectedly from last year's planting. Perhaps that's the most wonderful thing about spring, the discovery that something is always just under the surface, waiting to burst forth.

Of course, there are also the weeds, but we won't go there.

It's easy to understand why many people get hooked on gardening. Certainly it's hard work, but the eventual beauty and bounty are so rewarding. There is nothing like stepping outside early in the morning, holding a fresh cup of coffee, to view the amazing results of all the waiting, hoping and hard work. At that moment, two thoughts invariably spring up: the knowledge that, though we did the work, it was God who caused the growth; and a better understanding of God's amazing renewal process in our own lives as well.

Suddenly we realize that somewhere down the row our faith has also grown by leaps and bounds.

Turning Over A New Leaf

Being a writer, what always amazes me is what lies just below the surface. Like every other part of life, writing has its more productive seasons—times when words tumble out almost unbidden. Much of the time, though, you have to dig for them. During the particularly unproductive spells you may even resort to exchanging seeds...oops, I mean ideas...with other writers. Even these ideas must often incubate for a while so that through you're not writing, you're still thinking about it, constantly nurturing what is germinating.

When you finally get down to the tired and tedious business of planting something on paper, it is often serendipitous what springs up. "Where in the world did that thought come from?" you exclaim. "I'm brilliant!"

But we know it's not we who are brilliant. It is the Lord who uses every season and experience of our lives to plant these seeds of faith and truth within us. Still, how thankful we all are when God causes a new season of growth to spring up in our hearts.

It was during one such season that God planted this poetic prayer in my heart:

> *Thank you, Lord, for new beginnings,*
> *Another year, a bit more time;*
> *A baby's birth, a glad reunion*
> *Morning's light, new heights to climb.*

Spring

Clear direction, so long sought for,
New doors opened by Your hand,
Marking yet another chapter
On the way that you have planned.

The hope You bring, the peace You promise,
Once realized, we're not the same.
For there is found a new beginning
Each time we whisper Jesus' name.

CHAPTER TWO

Spring Cleaning

Create in me a pure heart, O God, and renew a steadfast spirit within me.
—Psalm 51:10

Nothing reveals the strengths and weaknesses of a marriage like cleaning the garage. A recent collaboration on this task illuminated some cobwebs in both.

First I discovered that my husband is—gasp—a stacker. He actually believes a garage exists for the sole purpose of housing a vehicle. Thus, everything else need only be stacked around it.

I, to his dismay, am a strategist. Cleaning of this magnitude takes careful planning—in one case, six years. Was it my fault that just when I'd settled on the perfect plan we moved?

Thanks to Martha Stewart, I see a garage where everything is not only immaculate, but color-coded.

Spring

My husband contends that cardboard IS a color. Deluded man. Every Martha wannabe knows you need see-through containers with colored lids and cabinets for storing things...in alphabetical order.

I cannot prudently tell you where he suggested we file Martha.

Then there's sentiment. My husband is attached to the weirdest things—like golf clubs he no longer uses, each representing some special achievement. Once he announced he'd won a sand wedge. I thought he said 'sandwich' and couldn't quite grasp his excitement.

Okay. I, too, admit fault in this department. It seems every book, box and bag of memorabilia requires a coffee break, and box of tissue, to peruse. So what if I am occasionally sidetracked when finding forgotten treasures just pleading to be displayed? Necessitating something be moved. Revealing a need for cleaning, painting or wallpapering. Confirming my case for a bigger house...with a barn.

Alas, we do not live without clutter, humanly or spiritually. Clinging stubbornly to things of the past, we stack our baggage neatly, barely leaving God enough space. Or we present to Him our long-range plan for organizing life into manageable little compartments. Mercifully, when we can no longer circumvent the clutter, God schedules a work day and says "Let's sort it out together."

Why I can even imagine a heavenly color-coding system: righteous red for 'forgiven', misty white for 'forgotten', and spring green for 'new beginnings.'

Turning Over A New Leaf

We all have 'em—garages, closets and junk drawers where things just tend to accumulate. When we finally get around to tackling the mess, it's amazing to discover what's in there and why we kept it so long. Of course, we all know how much better we feel when we've tackled a messy room, drawer or closet. There's a satisfaction bordering on downright joy. *Now*, we think, *if we can just keep it that way.*

The same is true spiritually.

Sometimes, like the Psalmist, we ponder how God can live in our cluttered lives and why we continually allow things to take over and squeeze him out. But messes don't seem to bother God one bit. In fact he delights in taking the chaos and bringing it into order. The good news is if we are willing, He is able. All we have to do is ask. It was the philosopher, Horace, who said: *He has half the deed done who has made a beginning.* If we will only make a start, God will meet us in the messy middle.

> *Lord, how quickly our lives become cluttered to the point of confusion. Things just seem to accumulate before we know it. Our human attempts at organizing only seem to work for so long. Once we start shoving things back on the shelf, we know we're in trouble. We need help! Create a clean space in our hearts once more and a spirit of resolve to keep it that way. Amen.*

CHAPTER THREE

Time Change Challenge

My times are in your hands...
—Psalms 31:15

Somewhere towards the beginning of April the country makes a conscious and collective leap into spring. We call it Daylight Savings Time. Here's the concept. Move your clock ahead one hour and... voila! Everyone "springs forward" and gets an extra hour of evening light.

But wait just a hoppin' minute.

We also lose an hour's sleep. I don't know about you, but for me that constitutes jet lag.

Okay. I know it's only an hour's difference. Problem is it always starts in the morning. Whose idea was that? Even if the birds are chirping and the sun is shining, losing an hour's sleep just throws my time clock into a tizzy.

"So go to bed early," you say. Any finely calibrated person knows that doesn't work. I can't go to sleep at ten o'clock when my body thinks it's only nine. Besides, isn't the idea to extend your day? Then, hello! Going to bed early sort of defeats the whole purpose.

Here's another clock-wise concern. To blindly and obligingly spring in any direction might pose a serious safety issue. Aren't we taught to look before we leap? Not jump to conclusions? Maybe we need to give this vernal vault more consideration.

Truth is I am one of those time-challenged people who can't afford to lose an hour. When you're always running behind—not to mention sleep deprived—losing time could have serious repercussions.

Eventually, of course, we all adjust. It's still twenty-four hours whether tacked on at the beginning or end. "Hour by hour," the Psalmist writes, "I place my days in your hands..."[2]

Interesting how times of change, tiny or tumultuous, can reflectively reinforce the importance of committing our days to God, asking Him to help us make the most of them.

So take heart, time travelers. Autumn will compensate our snooze time. In the meantime, waking or sleeping, God's presence fills our days. That's really all we need to 'fall back' on.

Turning Over A New Leaf

As long as we're talking time, here, let me take the opportunity to tackle a subject with which—judging from the number of articles in every major women's

---

[2]Psalm 31:15 The Message

magazine on eliminating stress, organizing your time...space...thoughts... yada, yada, yada—most women struggle. That is not having enough time. No wonder to think of losing one more hour in our already maxed-out day is, well, unthinkable.

Contrary to popular teaching the key is not just better time management or optimum organization. Certainly those things can be useful tools in eliminating the clutter from our schedules and spaces. However, based on responses I've received from a vast repertoire of women's retreats, plus my own experience attempting to balance the myriad responsibilities and expectations accompanying thirty-eight-plus years of marriage and ministry, I've come to another conclusion: Discipline only works long-term when it is spiritually motivated.

The best motivation for getting our lives in order is to truly understand how much God loves us, what a wonderful plan he has for our lives, and, if given a chance, how he will help us eliminate whatever interferes with it. Our days truly are in his hands. Let's commit them once more to God, asking him to help us make the most of them.

> *Lord, we need your help. We've gotten in such a routine of rushing that we forget the slow lane is not only still an option, but the better part of wisdom. Help us to place our time in your hands then stop trying to take it back. Amen.*

CHAPTER FOUR

May Mischief

And whatever you do, whether in word or deed, do it all in the name of the Lord Jesus, giving thanks to God the Father through him.
—Colossians 3:17

Anybody besides me old enough to remember May baskets? The ideas was on May 1st, or "May Day", you'd make little paper cones, fill them with flowers and hang them on someone's door knob. Then you'd knock, run like crazy, and hide to watch the recipient discover the surprise. It was a fun way to brighten someone's day and welcome spring.

No one seems to celebrate May Day anymore. After all we don't know our neighbors that well and in this day you could get shot running off someone's porch, hiding in their bushes. Imagine the headlines: "Crazed Woman Brandishing Basket of Begonias

Spring

Blasted By Birdshot." Maybe it's no longer worth the risk.

I know of a church youth group who responded to a sermon about committing random acts of kindness by doing nice things in their community, expecting nothing in return. Like handing out balloons in a local park and holding a free car wash. They even went downtown and fed coins into parking meters about to expire. This caused trouble because the city wasn't making any money on parking tickets. Obviously kindness is in the eye of the recipient.

Still, there are so many ways to brighten someone's life if we just take time. How about "hanging" baskets filled with kind words and encouragement? Lend a listening ear; share an idea, scripture, or inspirational article.

Even a smile becomes a welcome "basket" to someone who doesn't expect it—like the check stand clerk who's having a really bad day.

How about writing an appreciative note to someone you love? When my sons entered the touchy teenage years, writing became a safer form of communication, giving us time to choose words and respond in a thoughtful way.

Looking back, it was the joyous surprise of May Day that I treasure. I've revised a familiar saying: "God works in mischievous ways, His wonders to perform." Bless someone today, then step back and enjoy the mischief!

Turning Over A New Leaf

It was Ralph Waldo Emerson who wrote, *You cannot do a kindness too soon, for you never know how soon it will be too late.* This statement has never been truer than in today's fast-paced world with its complex and confusing issues. Certainly we need to touch and influence as many lives as we can while there is still time. What better reason to get in the habit of committing random acts of kindness, of doing everything with excellence and passion.

Will it really make a difference? we sometimes wonder. I believe any time, in any way that we express love and compassion in the name of Jesus, we have made a difference in that person's life. Someone once said that people may never remember all the things you say, but they will never forget what you do.

Maybe some of us feel like all we do is encourage and support others, leaving little time left over for ourselves. It might help to think that in some small way, the accomplishments of everyone whom our lives touch in some significant way are our own accomplishments as well.

> *Lord, it's so easy in the busy and bothersome world we live in to get self-centered and forget how much healing there is in even the smallest act of kindness. Make us more aware of the needs and feelings of others. Help us take the time to reach out, to touch someone for your sake. Amen.*

CHAPTER FIVE

Happy Mother's Day

Can a mother forget the baby at her breast and have no compassion on the child she has borne?
—Isaiah 49:15

When it comes to having kids, here's one of my favorite quotes from author Barbara Johnson: "If raising children was supposed to be easy, it wouldn't have started with something called labor."[3]

Every mother knows, by then it's too late to back out.

I do have one frazzled friend who, grasping at straws, admitted having days when she wished someone would hurry up and figure out how to make birth control retroactive.

---

[3]Barbara Johnson, *Highlights from So Stick A Geranium In Your Hat and Be Happy* (Word Publishing, 1993) 62

Let's be honest, moms. We've all had times of wondering whether life might not have been simpler had we chosen to remain single or childless.

No question, families are a full-time job.

Part of the problem lies in not knowing what may surface in the gene pool. Take our three boys, for instance. A Mother's Day card I received when they were young, which—judging from the flowery front—their dad picked out, clearly demonstrates their different personalities:

Challenging Oldest Child: *Happy Mom's day! Things are getting better, thanks for putting up with me.*

(There's a choice?)

Middle Kid Possessing Literary Flair: *Mom, it would be foolish to try to put into words how much I love and appreciate you. I hope that instead my actions will be able to emulate what I'm sure you already know.*

(And that starts when?)

Laid-back youngest: *Happy Mother's day!! Have a nice day off!*

(I'm still waiting.)

Truth is, we learn more about God through family dynamics than any other earthly relationship—trust, intimacy, commitment, unconditional love, and long suffering, just to name a few.

Still need a bit of encouragement? Psalms 127:3 reminds us that "children are a gift of the Lord" and "a reward."

So on the days when you're tempted to return the gift, focus on the rewards—like grandchildren. And feel free to liberally employ another favorite quote that recently came across my e-mail: "Grandchildren are our reward for allowing our own children to live."

Happy day, Moms! Hope the humor helps.

Turning Over A New Leaf

Without a doubt, my mother was the single most significant influence of my life. She was a model homemaker who cooked, sewed and kept an immaculate home. Even though she periodically worked outside the home, she somehow still managed to participate in my many activities and interests. This was especially amazing considering she was 40 years old when I was born. Yet if she ever felt old, she certainly never acted it or looked it. She kept up with current fashions and taught me all the beauty secrets she knew. "You're as young as you feel" was the motto she modeled.

Now that Mom has gone to heaven, hardly a day goes by that something doesn't remind me of her, but especially spring flowers. She loved them and had them everywhere. Spring was a special time when she waited to see if what she had planted would come to life.

What I didn't really think about until I became a parent, and now as a grandparent watching my children raising their children, is how parents also plant spiritual seeds, some of which take many seasons to see bloom. It's what I now call the time-released principle of Christian training, knowing that under the right conditions and at just the right time, it is God, the Master Gardener, who will cause them to bloom.

So, don't be discouraged if you feel like nothing you say or do seems to be taking root in your children's lives. Keep planting those seeds. Do your best and God will do the rest.

Lord, sometimes being a parent really is a thankless task. No one knows that better than you. Give us the patience to keep planting and the faith to believe that we will eventually see our children blossom, trusting you for the time it takes to see them become rooted. Amen.

CHAPTER SIX

New Lease on Life

Teach us to number our days that we may have a heart of wisdom.
—Psalm 90:12

I don't know a woman alive who looks forward to her annual physical exam. Just the word *exam* conjures up nightmares for me. Will I pass? How do you study for a physical? And what does a C- translate to, health-wise?

I'll soon find out.

Sitting on the edge of the cushioned, paper-covered examination table, I study my dangling toes. *Yep... definitely time for a pedicure.* Say, maybe I should postpone the exam until I can get one.

Too late. I'm here. May as well get it over with.

As the fluorescent light reflects off a metal tray of shiny instruments, a shiver runs up my spine. Why are these rooms always so cold? Maybe it's part of the heart exam. A shivery stethoscope could certainly give you a jump start. Or cause cardiac arrest.

The one-size-fits-none paper robes with the back draft don't help. Suddenly a favorite phrase of my mother's comes to mind—naked as a jaybird. What I wouldn't give now for a few well-placed feathers.

What's that? Footsteps and muffled voices outside the door and a scrape as my chart is lifted from its holder. Despite the chill, my palms start to sweat. Suddenly the door flies open and in walks a huge, scary guy in a white lab coat.

Eeeek!

Oh. It's Dr. Wong. He's not scary. And, actually, he's short.

"Hi, Judi. How're you doing?"

My tension spills over. "I've tried, Doc. I really have! I'm exercising three times a week, trying to make healthy food choices and eliminate stress. But sometimes I blow it. Is there hope, Doc? Am I gonna make it?"

He smiles. "Relax. Let me ask a few questions, then we'll run some routine tests. I'm sure everything is fine."

And it was. Thank you, Lord.

Like I said, every woman alive should look forward to her annual exam. Life is short, after all. Isn't it worth being given another year's lease on life?

Turning Over A New Leaf

Is there a woman alive who actually looks forward to her annual physical exam? Probably not, but she should. The problem is that because our natural tendency as women to nest and nurture causes us to take on the caregiver role for everyone else we often end up neglecting ourselves. The obvious question, then, should be, "If something happens to us, who will take over that role?"

Still we keep going, thinking we can do it all and often underestimating—or not wanting to admit—our own limitations. Certainly there is no limit to what a determined woman can accomplish. The question is, at what cost? Like it or not, it's a biblical fact that God created Eve as a help mate and co-creator. There is a reason women are built differently, think differently, and are emotionally and physiologically "wired" and "plumbed" differently than men. We need to take care of that delicate wiring and plumbing.

For our own good we need to pay attention to our inward whispers for equilibrium. That means knowing our own personal physical and emotional limitations, seeking God's direction, then taking on only the tasks that nurture and support our physical, emotional and spiritual wellbeing.

Life, at best, is short. That makes an annual renewal of our lease on it imperative.

Lord, your word says we are "fearfully and wonderfully made." Give us wisdom in understanding the delicate balance of our own mental, physical and emotional well-being. Help us to listen to our bodies and take care of them. We know you'd want us to. Amen.

CHAPTER SEVEN

Divine Design

She selects wood and flax and works with eager hands.
—Proverbs 31:13

In spring, poetically speaking, a young man's fancy turns to thoughts of love. For women, it's decorating. Something about the sunlight filtering through windows just makes our creative juices flow...usually as winter dirt marks show. Unbidden, some vernal volition to achieve a fresh, new look soon has us devouring catalogs and magazines for ideas. Proverbs 31-inspired, we stalwartly seek the most design for our dollar, paint for our peso, and bureau for our euro.

Hence we arise one morning before the light reveals the lint to look (blearily) well to the ways of our household. Once the household is shoved—lovingly—out the door, we grab our dog-eared decorating

Spring

magazine and head for the nearest mega-discount, do-it-yourself home store. We've arrived at a divine design! Undoubtedly something subconsciously involving wool, flax, linen, scarlet and purple in one form or another.

At the risk of seeming unspiritual, allow me some personal observations.

Do you realize how many colors of scarlet there are? Named after flowers, fruits or vegetables? Logically, then, one *should* blend harmoniously with eggplant. Uh-uh. Just try sleeping in a red and purple room. We're talking instant insomnia.

And what exactly is flax? I doubt you'd want sheets made from it...or wool either.

Linen, however, has possibilities. Recently I spied the perfect bedspread...linen-look, machine washable, ON SALE. A soothing floral print, it included every conceivable coordinating accessory. Things were coming together until I impulsively ordered paint to match one small flower. The resulting revelation: beige is a choice, but vintage rose is a commitment.

Thankfully, unwise decisions in life, decorating or otherwise, can usually be forgiven or corrected. In God's Divine Design, they serve as valuable lessons to help us make better future choices.

So don't throw in the swatch.

Oh, and remember...there's no accounting for personal taste. Once, going for a certain "look", I hung mosquito netting over the bed. That night my confused husband asked, "So, is this supposed to be romantic?"

"How do you feel?" I purred.

"Itchy."

Turning Over A New Leaf

Here are a couple of things I've learned about styles and seasons. First, what goes around once usually comes around again, just in some different form or fabric. Second, though some things last only for a season, every season teaches us something. The hope is that we learn enough from each not to repeat the same mistakes twice.

Of course some things, life-wise and otherwise, are simply more obvious than others. Take that unfortunate plaid, polyester leisure suit phase from the 1970's, for instance. Who'd want to repeat a mistake like that? Other things in our lives are mandated by maturity. While I find a few of today's youthful styles appealing, there's no way at my age and weight I'd be caught dead in some of 'em. The older I get, the more I realize there are some things, style-wise and otherwise, God knows I just don't wear well. Like bitterness, for instance.

It's the things that aren't as obvious which we are continually having to sort out. But don't get discouraged. Sometimes you've got to try on a lot of different styles before you know what works for you. It's all part of becoming the person God created you to be. Remember, He really does have a divine design for our lives.

Lord, life sometimes seems like a process of trial and error. Most times it's fun, but many other times frustrating. Looking back we can see that we've come a long way in sorting it all out. Help us avoid any major future mistakes in judgment by seeking the divine design you have for our lives. Amen.

CHAPTER EIGHT

Squeaky Clean

You are already clean because of the word I have spoken to you.
—John 15:3

It started as a routine stop on a fine spring day. My friend, Karissa, and I were running errands when I noticed my car's fuel gage near empty. Spotting a gas station, I swerved in, filled the tank, then impulsively pushed the complimentary drive-through car wash button. *After all, what says 'spring' better than a squeaky clean car?*

Famous last thoughts.

Code entered, the words, "Drive forward" flashed green, luring us into the cool, damp tunnel until "Stop!" screamed its red warning. Turning off the motor provided momentary silence before everything flew into motion. Whirr. Swish. Soon

Spring

we sat engulfed in a sudsy cyclone, peering blurrily through the soap-streaked windshield. Then...

WHOOSH!

Two behemoth-sized brushes dropped down, heading straight for us. We both jumped, then embarrassed, giggled. As car wash veterans we knew this was normal. No need to panic.

Yet.

No sooner had the brushes hit the windshield than everything stopped. Drip...drip...drip. Thirty seconds passed...forty-five. Nothing.

Karissa spoke first. "I think it's stuck."

"Or caught on something," I replied hopefully. "Roll down your window and take a look."

No sooner had she done so, than like some crazed sea creature, the brushes' soggy strips flipped inside the car. Shrieking, Karissa poked them back out and rolled up the window.

Not only were we stuck—there were monsters out there! Our dauntless detour had turned suddenly scary. We needed help.

Karissa, bless her, climbed over the seat and out the back door. Three minutes later—from a safe distance—she shouted the station attendant's solution. "You'll have to back your car out."

Sure...right over the six cars behind me.

Amazing, isn't it, how quickly what appears harmless in life can become so complicated? Lured in easily, we soon find ourselves with blurred vision, trapped in a confining tunnel of confusion.

Thank goodness there's divine deliverance.

Isaiah 1:18 gives us the escape plan: "Come now let us reason together, says the Lord. Though your sins are like scarlet, they shall be as white as snow."

Now that, friend, is squeaky clean.

Turning Over A New Leaf

Ever notice how quickly in life something that seems so routine can develop into a dire dilemma? Undoubtedly we've all experienced it to one degree or another. One fine day we're going about our business and suddenly find ourselves in some sticky situation, one we never anticipated. Is it because we did something wrong or should have known better? No, it's because "life," in the words of an old song, "is what happens when we're making other plans."

Still it can be somewhat disconcerting, even scary. Isn't it wonderful to know that even in the unexpected circumstances of life, God's already got us covered? If you want some scriptural reassurance, just read Psalms 91. I especially like verse 11: "For he will command his angels concerning you to guard you in all your ways." That is just one small part of the many wonderful words he has spoken over us.

Lord, thank you for your Word that is full of promises concerning us. We're so grateful. There is provision in it for every problem of life, expected or unexpected. That means no matter how grimy life gets, we're can't help but come out squeaky clean. Amen.

CHAPTER NINE

The Vernal Pool

There is a time for everything, and a season for every activity under heaven."
—Ecclesiastes 3:1

Our new home sits directly across the street from a vernal pool. What, you will surely ask, is a vernal pool? To be honest, I wasn't sure either. I had to look it up. It is not a body of water as the name suggests, but rather an area reserved and protected for whatever animal and plant life lives and grows there. Trusting that the surrounding neighborhood would offer the same amenities to its "people life," we bought the house. Mostly, though, I loved looking out the windows at the open space.

We moved in at the end of November, locating the boxes marked 'decorations' just in time to produce something that resembled Christmases we have known and loved. It wasn't until late January that I was finally able to look up from my decorating magazines long enough to closely examine what lay immediately beyond the front door. What met my view was a vast lumpy field full of rangy brown grass encompassed by a dark chain link fence. At that moment I pondered whether we had made the wisest choice of location.

As for animal life, all I ever saw were birds—most of them little brown birds that blended into the overall color scheme so that you didn't see them so much as hear them. Occasionally a lone brown hawk circled the field looking, I imagined, for little brown mice. In other words, everything at that moment looked, well, brown. Add to that the lonely whistle of the train cutting across the far side of the field and the winter rain producing a wet hay smell and you have a rather bleak picture.

That is when I decided to look up the word 'vernal' in the dictionary. The definition stated simply: "of, relating to, or occurring in the spring." Spring being a few months away, I went back to the activities of my busy household.

Just a few months prior to the move, my son, daughter-in-law and grandson, Liam, had come from Oregon to live with us in order to ease my son's completion of a teaching degree. We were just getting used to having an active four-year-old in the house, when my daughter-in-law made the announcement that a new baby was expected in the spring. What a pleasant surprise.

Spring

Pleasant surprise? Who am I kidding? It was the worst timing in the world and we were all in an initial state of shock. How is it that despite our new century ability to regulate these things, babies still never come when it's financially feasible or chronologically convenient? And, unfortunately in the brown, bleak world around us, a lot of them suffer for it.

The adjustment was hardest, perhaps, for my son whose immediate goals seemed in jeopardy facing the responsibility of a growing family. The fact is he was just beginning to chart a promising course after some rather difficult years. Eventually we all settled into the wait, though the tension of adjustment was evident.

Spring seemed like a long way off on all accounts.

Sometime in February Grampa and Liam started the routine of walking our two dogs in the field-that-will-be-a-park. One day Liam burst through the door with exciting news. "Gramma, we saw FOUR rabbits!" The great rabbit-counting adventure began. The brown lumpy field had become a wild safari seen through the eyes of a four-year-old.

The late spring rains began, the large white egrets came and my daughter-in-law took on the mysterious beauty of a lady-in-waiting. My son worked longer hours, studied late into the night and looked very tired. The marriage definitely showed signs of stress. Life in our household and the vernal pool

Simple Seasons

were both changing. The question still remained whether either would be for the better.

One night I couldn't sleep and got up to do what moms do best—pray and worry, not always in that order. Needing solitude, I stepped out onto the front porch and was met with the surprisingly loud brik-brik-brik of frogs coming from the vernal pool. I could not see them, but obviously they were there—the sound of life coming from the darkness. And I thought of the heartbeat of my unborn grandchild.

I have lived long enough to witness the cycle of many seasons—some very difficult—and to finally understand how necessary and integral they are to each other. Even the bleak times must be celebrated in the hope of what is to come. So also, the seasons of life.

Pondering that, a lesson from the vernal pool began to reveal itself: We can't always regulate or predict nature, but if we can lovingly protect it and give it a chance, it will grow and thrive. Suddenly I understood that God had brought my son and family to live with us through such a season. He makes no mistakes. This was but another opportunity to apply our faith and prove Him faithful.

On the April day that tiny, beautiful Olivia Roseanne came home from the hospital with her mom and dad, I sat at the top of the stairs looking out the transom window at the vernal pool.

By now it was a lush green carpet with serendipitous stripes of color—wildflowers of yellow and purple and orange and white. Life in the vernal pool—and our home—had come full circle. I had seen the look on my son's face as his new daughter made her way into the world and watched now as he sat on the couch holding the tiny pink-wrapped bundle in his strong arms.

I thought of Ecclesiastes 3:1 which inspired the words of a favorite old song:

In His time, in His time,
He makes all things beautiful In His time.
Lord, please teach me everyday,
As You're showing me Your way,
That You'll do just what You say, In Your time.

And through every season, He will.

www.ingramcontent.com/pod-product-compliance
Lightning Source LLC
Chambersburg PA
CBHW030326080526
44584CB00012B/736